Facts of Life

Volume 1:

In the Beginning

by *Nada-Yolanda*

MARK-AGE
Pioneer, Tennessee, USA

Quotation of the Dalai Lama from *The Good Heart.*
© 1996 by His Holiness the Dalai Lama.
© 1996 by World Community for Christian Meditation.
Courtesy of Wisdom Publications, 199 Elm Street, Somerville, MA 02144, USA.

$\frac{4}{0}$ 3

E-mail: iamnation@aol.com
Website: http://www.islandnet.com/~arton/markage.html

ISBN 0-912322-56-X
Library of Congress Catalog Card Number: 98-86286

FIRST EDITION

Manufactured in the United States of America
by Quebecor Printing, Inc., Kingsport, Tennessee

CONTENTS

Facts of Life

Volume 1:

In the Beginning

INTRODUCTION

FACTS OF LIFE FOR THE GOLDEN ERA

At this dawn of a new millennium, heralding the Golden Age of Aquarius, we are just beginning to comprehend the basic "facts of life" for successful spiritual living on Earth. What are these facts? They are the fundamental precepts, the universal principles, that the spiritual sages and avatars of all major religions and philosophies have taught and demonstrated since time immemorial.

Now, having reached a cosmic turning point of spiritual evolution, humanity must awaken to these truths. Every man, woman and child on Earth is being prodded, from Spirit within, to advance rapidly into a new dimension of spiritual expression. *Now is the time.*

Since 1960 we have been passing through a forty-year cycle of transition, a time of purification and preparation prior to our entrance into the Golden Era of peace, love and brotherhood. These are the long-prophesied Latter Days, the harvest period, the so-called War of Armageddon between the forces of light and darkness within each one's soul.

This planetary transition is the biblical alert known as "signs of the times" or the age of marks, or Mark Age period and program, when all who are perceptive can read clearly those obvious signals which herald the end of humanity's preoccupation with materiality and the beginning of its predominating sense of true spirituality, called fourth dimensional consciousness. But to pass through this planetary crisis successfully, we each must face the age-old dilemma of the soul, and choose: either to remain self-centered, selfish and uncaring; or to center ourselves on our spiritual Self, the I Am, and to serve all equally, by being *love in action.*

By choosing to be love in action, we shall accomplish this personal and planetary transmutation, and shall cross over safely into

1

the New Age. We shall prepare ourselves and all life on Earth for the Second Coming, expected around the year 2000.

The Second Coming is twofold: the second coming of each child of God into awareness of the spiritual, I Am, high Self, that divine spark within; and the return of the spiritual ruler or Prince of Earth, known as Sananda on the higher realms, but who is the same Master who incarnated as Moses, Elijah, Zarathustra, Gautama Buddha, Socrates and, lastly, as Christ Jesus of Nazareth.

At the appropriate time, which Spirit alone can determine, Sananda will fulfill his two-thousand-year-old promise to redescend from the etheric or Christ realms in his light body, the same resurrected form in which he ascended as Jesus of Nazareth. That infusion of light, to be experienced by all, will help lift every one of us and all life forms on Earth into cosmic awareness, and thereby will inaugurate the two thousand years of Aquarius. The time has come for our spiritual graduation into the next schoolroom of life.

I AM NATION

To prepare for this personal and planetary event, all light workers on Earth are being inspired consciously and/or subconsciously to externalize the I Am Nation. The I Am Nation is a congregation, or networking, of all souls on the planet who give allegiance, first and foremost, to God and the I Am Self of each other person.

The I Am Nation is a prototype for spiritual government of, for and by the I Am Selves of all people on Earth. *It is not a political organization.* Regardless of religion, philosophy, gender, race, nationality, profession, or social status, everyone is a potential I Am Nation citizen.

Thus the I Am Nation is not a geographical place. It is a pledge of consciousness and actions. I Am Nation citizens are those who think, feel and act as spiritual beings in a physical body. They are striving unconditionally to be the Christ or I Am Self. They automatically are a network of light which circles the globe sending and receiving the thoughts of *peace, love, cooperation and coordination:* the keynotes of the dawning Aquarian Age. They radiate these spiritual thoughts to every living creature on our beloved planet Earth.

They are quiet families and homes, schools, communities. They

2

NADA-YOLANDA & EL MORYA/MARK
We were keynote speakers at the 1962 Oakland Space Convention

work in every business, profession and public service where they strive to bring equality, fairness, higher standards into every aspect of their efforts here and now.

There is no formal membership or dues to learn how to evolve deliberately into unified citizens of the I Am Nation. But Mark-Age, Inc., a nonprofit spiritual-educational organization founded in 1960, has been commissioned by the Hierarchal Board, or spiritual government of our solar system, to be the physical coordinating headquarters to help network those who wish to be linked on Earth as the I Am Nation.

Originally located in Miami, then in Ft. Lauderdale, Florida, we now operate in Elk Valley, Tennessee, north of Knoxville. Our five divisions are: *I Am Nation News* (quarterly magazine), I Am Network of Light (weekly cassette meditation program which is broadcast internationally by centers, churches, study groups and individuals), University of Life, Healing Haven, and Centers of Light.

TEACHINGS OF UNIVERSITY OF LIFE

As soon as we began operations in 1960, El Morya/Mark (1922–1981) and I, cofounders of Mark-Age, realized the need for materials that would introduce the higher possibilities of spiritual living on Earth. Truth seekers–beginners and advanced students alike–thirsted for teaching tools they could use to work effectively with the changing conditions of our world.

To this end, via our University of Life and other divisions, we have published a plethora of books, booklets, courses, periodicals and audiocassettes, based on the numerous channeled communications and inspirations Mark and I, as well as others of our United Staff, have received from our I Am Selves and from the ascended masters of celestial (angelic), etheric, and higher astral realms.

In the late 1960s and early 1970s, we released a series of brochures that gave the basic facts of life that all I Am Nation citizens needed to understand about this critical planetary changeover into the fourth dimension. Immediately these brochures, disseminated throughout the world, became popular both to introduce family and friends to metaphysical concepts and to refresh one's own insight into cosmic consciousness.

Since those days, we have foreseen the need to update and to reintroduce these easy-to-understand teachings. As an invaluable spiritual guidebook, *Facts of Life* addresses this need.

This first volume, "In the Beginning," therefore covers elementary spiritual topics of interest to all I Am Nation citizens, ranging from meditation to karma and reincarnation, to channeling and spiritual discernment. Also, El Morya/Mark introduces the metaphysical interpretation of biblical scriptures. Reverend Francis Cuzon, a Roman Catholic priest, gives insight into how Latter-Day changes are transforming one major religion.

Future volumes of *Facts of Life* will encompass spiritual teachings of intermediate and advanced levels in the University of Life.

The Age of Aquarius is dawning. Prepare yourself for the second coming of cosmic consciousness for each and every child of our Father-Mother God. Apply these simple facts of life–these timeless truths for enlightened, spiritual living on Earth. *Be love in action now!*

4

MEDITATION

Definition:

The process by which you may unite with your I Am Self

WHY?

Why should you develop and practice meditation? The answer is: in order to come into conscious communion with your spiritual, I Am or high Self. The I Am Self is that pure essence of God that is part of each one of us. The essence of God is in all things, for God or Spirit is the Creator of all that is.

As one of God's creations, man must discover that body, mind, soul and spirit are complex, but integrated. He has to learn to sort them out by seeking within, through concentration in meditation.

When you are able to contact the high Self within, the spiritual or God part, you can communicate with and contact everything that has Spirit within, be it man, animal, vegetable or mineral.

Spirit is the fundamental fact of life, your contact with your life. Wherever Spirit is, you can communicate with It. All of us have recognized or have sensed this communion at such times as when walking in the woods, gazing at the stars or holding a loved one in our arms. The joy of oneness with something outside of ourselves is only a hint of the fulfillment available to all.

All questions or problems can be answered or solved through meditation. By tuning in with Universal Mind, or Spirit, there is the knowledge and the power to do all things. This is the source of inspiration and ideas for that which you do every day in all of your activities. With meditation developed to various degrees, you become more tuned in with, and more receptive to, guidance in your everyday needs as well as help with particular problems.

Spirit works in strange and seemingly devious ways. This is to say that the answers to questions in meditation can become known in the most unexpected manner. Never limit Spirit by outlining what you think the answer should be. Spirit is much more generous in Its unlimited ways than you can possibly anticipate or expect. The enlightenment that comes in answer to your question is often overwhelming.

For example, sometimes you may not receive a conscious answer to a question, but nevertheless the problem will be solved. Or, you may receive an answer by a thought seemingly coming to you from nowhere when you are doing or thinking something else. You may be led to a certain book, or overhear a conversation or suddenly look up and see a signboard that will unveil your answer through a whole new train of thought. Sometimes no answer indicates that no answer is the answer.

You must try to keep from concentrating too hard, as that can tighten you and stop or block the flow of Spirit. There are times when Spirit protects you by not allowing you to gain certain information until you are developed enough to use it selflessly and for Spirit's purposes.

So you see a few things that can be gained through the practice of meditation. It is the first fact of eternal life, your first step of spiritual growth. Without step one you never get to step two. You learn to walk before you can run. Meditation is the foundation of self-unfoldment.

After you have developed the habit of daily practice you soon will achieve an understanding as to who, why, what and where you are. This will bring you clearly into the realization that you truly are an instrument of God. You will see and will understand that you are a small part of Spirit manifested here upon the Earth, and thereby have the joyful responsibility to do and to act as Spirit within you would have you do.

As a tuned-in spiritual instrument, you then can begin to do something constructive for our Father-Mother God. Now more than ever you must seek to increase your ability to receive divine ideas and direction. This will allow better use of your own divine power, to put it into effect, or to work, here in the physical and mental realms.

With the use of positive thinking and with your abilities to make decrees and by holding to your inspirations you can and do manifest these thoughts into existence to benefit yourself and all mankind. Having something come into your life is much more satisfying than just thinking about it and wishing it were so.

This is one of the major reasons you are learning of your spiritual nature: to aid in bringing enlightenment and physical changes upon Earth in a spiritual manner. This is an important function of all seekers of truth. You are learning to become your Self. When you become one with your I Am Self, your real Self, then and only then will you know and accomplish your purposes for being here upon this planet in this time of great need.

HOW?

How do you meditate? There is no one way or technique that is better than others. Each individual has a way of his/her own, best suited for him/her. It merely requires practice to find and to determine that way. It is presumed you are serious in your search and are eager to put forth the effort to do this, as the results are equal to your application.

That is primarily what the various techniques are meant to do. They are a starting point, an aid, to get you to begin practicing so you more easily can begin finding your own way. There are those who have said: I could meditate better before I began using a certain given technique. Be discerning in this matter. A given tech-

Meditate to commune with I Am Self
Painting courtesy of Arthur Douët

nique is to be used as a guide only, but is not to be leaned upon completely. The basic points that apply to everyone are as follows:

First, you must be comfortable and learn how to relax the mind and the body. Practice is necessary, and the sooner you start the sooner you will have results. A few deep breaths and some simple exercises to get the kinks out of the spine and neck will be of great help in relaxing the body. Stretching smoothly like a cat is most soothing. Take a sitting position, with the back or spine straight up and down. This can be done either sitting on the floor or in a chair.

With the hands folded or open palms upwards on the thighs, eyes closed, you can further relax by checking over each section and, if tensed, relax it. You can make a game of this by talking to each part, as: right foot, you are relaxed; right leg, you have been tense but now you are relaxed; and so forth. Soon you will learn to do this automatically.

To relax the mind, concentrating on an imaginary screen just inside the forehead or repeating silently a single word such as *Om* will help to eliminate the passing parade of thoughts. *Om* is a universal sound and carries peaceful, elevating vibrations.

Many times you suddenly will realize you are busy thinking about outside things and must redirect your thoughts to a single effort. You must guard your thoughts carefully at first. Many find calming the mind to be difficult, but, as with all things, practice and determination bring success.

Second, when finally relaxed, quieted and comfortable, send out a prayer, such as the Lord's Prayer or any personal favorite. This is to state your intention and attitude for meditation. It is most important to have a heart full of love and selfless giving. You may say it in your own words, but you are rededicating and giving yourself to God and are willing to accept that which you receive. Spirit gives unto you only as you give of yourself. As you sow, so shall you reap. The more you give the more you will receive, in order to keep the cup full. This is another fact of life, one of Spirit's laws.

Third, you must learn how to protect yourself. When you open to receive in meditation, especially if you are psychic but untrained, you could be visited by less desirable contacts of no particular aid to your development. There is a simple but effective protection, which is seeing yourself filled with and surrounded by the white light of truth.

You literally create an impenetrable force field of such a powerful vibration that none but those of the highest realms can enter. This is an important technique that is not commonly known, but hearing of it for the first time makes it usable to you immediately.

It is a simple thing to do. Merely visualize yourself in a cocoon of brilliant white light. See yourself wrapping or spinning it counterclockwise about you, closed at the bottom but with a small opening at the top. This opening provides direct contact with your I Am Self.

You may use the white light anytime during your daily activities when you feel the need for divine aid for yourself. You also may project white light to another for his or her protection. It is good to do this for yourself every day upon arising in the morning and before retiring at night, until this too becomes an automatic action.

Fourth, the act of meditation itself should be made up of two sections, equally important: projecting outwardly and receiving inwardly. When you project outwardly you see yourself as a transmitter of Spirit, sending out vibrations of peace, love

Wrap yourself in white light
Drawing courtesy of Gerry Libonati

and healing energies to those in need. You also can project to world situations of strife or calamity, and thus be an important calming and healing force.

Thoughts are things: another basic fact of life. Loving thoughts do good things to all they touch. You must be careful not to send thoughts of what you personally think should be done, but rather ask that Spirit handle the situation for the good of all concerned. No matter how big or how personal the problem may be, remember to say to Spirit: *Not my will, but Thy will be done.*

When you have finished the projection, you must learn to still all thoughts and to sit quietly and receptively. As a last thought, you might say something like: if there be something Spirit would have me know at this time which will aid me in my development, I do most humbly await that idea. Then enjoy the peace that can follow. Keep a calm, quiet and highly expectant attitude. If you expect nothing, that is exactly what you may receive.

After a period of practice you may receive sights or sounds that are common to many beginning students. You may hear your name called, which is one way the I Am Self tries to get your attention and interest. Faces may appear, which is a good introduction to receiving from another plane or dimension. Or, you could be making mental contact with another individual on this plane.

Vivid colors often are seen, in the form of rays or balls. This is the seeing of energy being directed toward you as stimulating or helpful vibrations. Another common first vision is that of seeing an eye. This is generally the third eye, seen by some as a tunnel. Some meditators can merge with the eye, or can travel through the tunnel to other planes and levels.

Some things seen or heard may have no apparent meaning. These should be filed for future reference, as additional disclosures at a later date could tie in and could help explain the puzzle. It is advisable to keep a notebook handy and to make a record. Much will be more meaningful when you can look back with greater understanding.

It is important to know that everyone does not hear voices or see some sort of vision when meditating. Such are pleasurable, but meditations are just as rewarding without them. The reasons for receiving these phenomena are generally as an aid to one's spiritual growth or as steps in psychic development. A strong vision often is used to get a borderline believer over the fence and on the path.

Many get their answers by just *knowing*. They have thoughts and ideas that suddenly come into the consciousness, and they accept and act upon them. They need no other type of convincing, and can take strength in that fact.

A calm, peaceful and joyous meditation is rewarding in itself; and much good comes in such, whether you are aware of it or not. Most of humankind still is unconscious of the love and energies that constantly are being sent to us from the higher realms. It is to each one's best interest to meditate often and deeply for spiritual awakening and unfoldment.

WHEN?

When is the best time to meditate? Any time of the day or night is good, but it is well to initiate and to cultivate the habit at certain times. This gets your system and mind used to the idea of daily application, of checking in with your high Self. Good habits never have to be broken. Many find the best times of the day to meditate are the first thing upon arising in the morning, while the mind is still calm and rested, and just before retiring at night, when there is a stopping of the day's activities and one can relax.

Another good time to meditate, and a good habit to cultivate, is to sit for five minutes every day at noon. This is an excellent time to practice projecting love and peace outwardly to the entire world, or to any part of it in particular that might come to your attention. You would be joining many other persons and groups all over the world who sit at noon, their time, to do this.

People from all faiths and philosophies are unified at this time to perform a vital function for Spirit. The cushion of love that is built up fills a great need for the planet and all upon it. Much good thus is accomplished for Earth on many levels and in many aspects. This is *love in action.*

The length of time you sit in meditation is optional. When you first begin to practice, ten minutes can seem an eternity. When you become accomplished at tuning in, an hour can be too short. For busy persons, fifteen minutes upon arising each day can be most beneficial. It gives time to rededicate one's self to Spirit's works, to project love to all, and to receive energy and ideas to enhance and to give direction to one's activities for the entire day.

Each individual eventually will come to his or her own ideal length of meditation period; which of course will vary for different times, based on need, degree of development and general circumstances. To sit for too short a period will not accomplish much, and the restlessness from sitting too long can nullify effectiveness.

EXPERIMENTS

Seeing is believing. Though we can get much helpful advice and direction from others, each must see it and learn it in his or her own fashion. There are many areas in which we can experiment and prove the value of meditation. For example, suppose you select a tree as the object of meditation. By concentration on this one single object you will discover that your thoughts expand and become illumined.

Realize that each individual part of the tree—the leaves, the roots, the branches and so forth—is an integral part of the whole, and that each part is dependent on all the other parts for its very life. Further meditation can show that, like the tree, all kinds of life are linked together and are dependent upon each other in one manner or another.

It is not likely that two people meditating on the same object will have the same illumination. One person meditating on a tree suddenly saw it as a bolt of solid lightning. Since all things are forms of energy vibrations, he saw the tree as a form of stopped motion, and gained insight and understanding as to the world of relativity.

You may select more abstract subjects and gain insight in a different manner. If you select a line from a letter you have received, you may gain intuitive knowledge as to the intended meaning or the inner thought the person had when writing it. If you work on understanding others' good and bad points, you could determine how to develop or to overcome them, respectively, within yourself.

Through these applied meditations on any subject you can gain new insight and expand your conscious awareness much more. That is the basic reward of these efforts, for through meditation you find that self-realization, understanding and comprehension are expanded and clarified as if a floodgate had been opened suddenly. At this point you become more firmly anchored in Spirit and you grow, in many wondrous and rewarding ways.

THINKING SPIRITUALLY

PRONOUNCEMENT

All workers of light use the PROnouncement of light and truth principles, which is the proper constructive method to be used and taught by all forces of light, rather than the destructive methods practiced consciously or unconsciously by many.

There are those, of mortal consciousness primarily, who in that consciousness presume to tell God and His agents or light forces of the Christ consciousness how to deal with unawakened humanity.

Mark-Age, as all I Am Nation citizens, does not employ the denouncement method of indiscriminate attack against persons, organizations or concepts. This does not mean in any sense that workers of the light do not seek out and eliminate error wherever it is discovered and whenever it is within the function of their work.

ဆ

What would Christ Jesus of Nazareth—known also as Sananda, the Prince of Peace and of Love, and who is the spiritual ruler of the planet Earth—say and do concerning the elimination of error conditions which prevail throughout the world today? His way has remained ever the same. Here is what he delivered in an inter-dimensional communication on July 10, 1962, through me as a spokesperson for him and all the ascended masters of the spiritual government of our solar system:

"It is necessary to speak and to act in a spiritual consciousness that has with it a higher form of control and guidance than anything to be done, said or presented in physical manners or means. Your whole purpose is not to work from physical levels into spiritual understanding, but to bring about a spiritual realization that will effect a material result. So I, as well as others working in this field

13

and aspect of control, wish to remind you of your responsibilities and to direct your thoughts to bringing about this desired result.

"Should there be in your minds any doubt of what we speak of here, let me assure you of abortive attempts previously made on this plane and planet for thousands of years, to verify your truth in these matters. I am not content with the agents working in these fields, because they so easily slip into the opposite or negative respect for what they have vouchsafed to do before incarnating upon this plane for the present cycle of evolution.

"We cannot work with denouncement, but only with PRO-nouncement of what we desire in the result aspect. Therefore, as proponents of the light we must PROnounce that light and PROspect the light all through our entire existence. So I see it, so be it."

Sananda/Jesus of Nazareth here uses a tool frequently employed by the masters of the etheric or Christ planes: a play of sound or words. To strengthen his meaning, he plays with the prefix *pro-,* which means to be *for* something; or, as it would be used in the word *professional,* one who is a master of his subject.

ELIMINATE THE NEGATIVE

In his statement the master coordinator for the planet's evolvement into Christ-conscious awareness speaks forth clearly and plainly for all who have eyes to see, ears to hear and inclination to act in truth. He reminds all that history repeatedly has shown the futility of seeking to effect lasting and proper results by using only physical or mental counterattacks against that which is error, no matter what or where. The only acceptable and permanent corrective measure is to employ spiritual methods, bringing down into the material world these spiritual concepts of truth to replace those which are not truth, and thus not of reality.

How consuming and ineffective have been the countless attempts to combat non-reality, that which has not its base in spiritual truth; rather than to ignore, although not to be unaware of its transitory appearance and need to be eliminated, such non-truth. Concentrate on bringing forth truth. Where has man's focus of attention been: in eliminating that which is not desired, or in bringing forth that which is real, is truth and is desirable?

Sananda/Jesus further has pointed out the dangers inherent in the denouncement method of seeking to ferret out error. Many spiritual leaders or guides—ministers, philosophers, therapists—who came not to participate in this necessary elimination phase, as well as countless others who are not so evolved and do not know the law involved, have fallen victim to the error they sought to fight. For to whatsoever we give our attention, that is what we tend to bring about. The light workers came at this time to demonstrate and to bring forth the light, the truth, the reality of spiritual law.

The higher the evolvement in spiritual understanding, the greater the degree of manifestation or creating of that which we think; for *to think is to create.* Therefore, it behooves all who have developed this power of thought to a high degree to use it to see, and therefore to bringing forth, only that which is desired, not that which is to be eliminated. To think or to dwell upon the *error* conditions, of which we certainly are aware, is to strengthen them.

There are those workers in the present program to bring about Christ-conscious awareness on this planet whose function and purpose are to combat errors, whatever and wherever they are, on those levels. But allow them to fulfill their work on their level of understanding and evolvement, without forfeiting the higher training and understanding of those who are *of* the light, who *teach* the light and who are *to bring forth* the light. Each to his own mission.

Give God and His agents full credit not only for knowing the present, as well as past and future, conditions of man and of Earth but also for knowing how to bring about the divine plan and for having absolute power to bring it forth. Those agents whose work it is to bring about the destruction of error do so constructively, using spiritual understanding and methods, working in at-onement with other forces of Spirit which build up that which is good and replace that which is not.

EVOLUTION NOT REVOLUTION

God works by evolution, not by revolution. God is love, not hate. God does not wantonly destroy that which is good just to eliminate that which is of error. The purpose of evolution is to keep that which is good and to add to it, while eliminating that which is not

15

desirable. To this purpose are Mark-Age and the citizens of the I Am Nation dedicated in all things throughout the world and affairs of man. That which has merit shall be emphasized and shall be encouraged, while that which is not of truth will be replaced constructively and surely.

There are many constructive criticisms, pointings-out of error thinking, actions and methods. This chapter is a sample of such. But in Christlike manner of correction we state the spiritual principle involved and throw the light on the less-than-perfect manifestation of it in an individual, in an organization, in a nation, or in an idea.

It is by these ways and means that I Am Nation citizens throughout the world bring about the necessary evolutionary changes within the scope of the divine plan for the upliftment of all equally into I Am consciousness in these Latter Days, the judgment time prophesied in all religions, myths and philosophies. This is the preparation that includes both the total elimination of that which is not spiritual and the manifestation of that which is spiritual, for the return of the ruler of this planet, Jesus the Christ.

In these words we speak as representatives of Christ Jesus and the entire Hierarchy of ascended masters throughout our solar system. Use whatever form of divine power deemed proper by Spirit and the agents of Spirit who constitute the spiritual government of etheric (Christed) masters and angelic beings. But always the method of bringing about changes for spiritual purposes will be that of PROnouncement: the speaking of the positive word as *love in action.*

God's creations, including man, are constantly in a state of evolutionary change toward greater manifestation of His glory. Therefore, we must not think man's creations are exempt from such perfecting changes. All that exists on the physical Earth today is being changed for higher manifestation for the Golden Age.

That which is not of a certain divinely prescribed standard of spiritual value and potential will not be allowed to manifest on the Earth after approximately the year 2000 A.D. So, it behooves all who sincerely wish and work for the elimination of error from Earth today to recognize that it is God's plan and purpose to effect the necessary changes.

LET GO AND LET GOD

The next step is to accept the reality that God also knows how and when to bring about all necessary steps in this plan. Therefore, what is really needed by man, acting as the expresser of God on this plane, is to turn to Spirit and the agents of Spirit for the necessary plans and procedures to eliminate that which is decreed by Spirit to go, and to bring forth that which is to come.

Sometimes the concentration to bringing forth the desired and decreed manifestation automatically effects the elimination of that which is not of truth. We are agreed there is an overabundance of error thinking and conditions on the planet. This also means there is a tremendous shortage of light workers and light projects demonstrating what is to replace the error situations once we successfully have eliminated them. Light workers must *see* and *be,* so that what they see *will* be.

With this understanding of and cooperation with Spirit and the Hierarchy, light workers of, for and with the light of God's immutable laws, who are demonstrating I Am Nation principles, hereby make this clear and concise statement of positive, cooperative and spiritual evolutionary policy regarding such specifics as are currently under attack by those who should know better. Pledge now your constructive support of all those individuals, organizations and programs which truly seek to manifest the two basic rules for the Golden Age: *Love God and Love One Another.*

Where there are good policies, support them. Where there is need for change, also speak and act for such; with and in love giving forth the constructive or positive aspect, rather than denouncing to eliminate the negative aspect, all within the scope of your powers and your missions.

Support those governments and those organizations of religious, spiritual, educational and research nature, including churches, which desire to work for and to establish God's will and to eliminate man's tyranny over man, to the best of their understandings and abilities. This list is by no means intended to be complete, nor is blanket approval meant for all individuals and actions within such organizations or groups.

17

Citizens of the I Am Nation serve Spirit only, in whomever and whatever Spirit is able to bring forth Its plans. So we see it, so be it. Give your thanks for the glorious opportunity to participate in this planet's peaceful transition from a third dimensional or physical manifestation into a fourth dimensional or mental-spiritual understanding and expression of life.

PROJECT POWER

Here are the basic metaphysical steps followed by I Am Nation citizens around the globe in sending forth light where there is error; or, projecting power and love:

1. Pray without ceasing. This means to think positively at all times. In order to prepare the way for such continual positive thinking, you must eliminate all negative thinking from your own total consciousness, which includes both the conscious and the subconscious. When dwelling on or entertaining negative thoughts, you are not able to receive positive thoughts from Spirit or the agents of Spirit, which includes your own Christ or spiritual Self. You cannot think both positively and negatively on the same subject at the same time, so choose this day, and each day, which you will serve.

It has been said many times in many ways that peace must begin with the individual. There is a well-known inspired song that beautifully expresses this: *Let There Be Peace on Earth; Let It Begin with Me.* So, the first step toward the use of PROnouncement is to eliminate the error in your own thinking. For truly is the Battle of Armageddon now being waged. But it is a mental war, with the battleground being in the thoughts of each and every person on Earth.

Let each one of us therefore concentrate first, although not exclusively so, upon clearing out the error in our own cities, governments and organizations: *the groups of thoughts within our own consciousness.* When peace has been established in our own earth, then the crusade can be carried forth from a base of operations that will remain impregnable and calm regardless of the enemy camps into which you and I send forth our thought soldiers.

2. Be love. This is the primary weapon of all I Am Nation citizens and does not wait for peace to be established first. Error cannot withstand divine love, the love of God for each and all of His/Her creations. This love is always within man, ever ready for his use. We need not seek it, define it or manufacture it; *love is.* Always existing within each man, woman and child, and always ready to pour forth at his/her direction, it surmounts any and all obstacles.

Without using it, we not only are ineffective in elimination of error and in bringing forth that which is of Spirit but we also are unprepared to cope with the weapons which those of negative intent, be they individuals or forces, turn against us. Easily we fall into defeat, or most subtly and insidiously are manipulated so as to become a tool and an advocate of that which we started out to fight.

Therefore, become skilled in the use of the divinely given armor and weapon: love. The principle on which the spiritual Hierarchy carries out the plans of Spirit is *love in action.* Make this yours also.

3. Thy will, not mine, be done. One of our functions as co-creators with God is, when we see imbalance or error, to use our right and duty to ask Creative Spirit that proper balance be restored to that individual or situation, resulting in divine order and harmony according to the will of God. Many times what we decree in this manner will not come to pass as we think it should, but when we have fulfilled the function of asking for balance to be restored according to the will of God, we must let it so manifest. *Let go and let God.*

Within God's plan it may be that you are to do something further; then it will come to your attention. It may or may not be that you are to be an instrument in the bringing forth of the proper outcome. Never dilute pronouncements by indulging in negative thoughts or actions or by seeking to take the initiative from God.

Study the Lord's Prayer; it contains the seven basic steps for perfect harmony and balance on Earth as they are in heaven (the Christed or angelic realms). Practice the Golden Rule: *Do to others as you would have them do to you.* At all times enact the two commandments for entry into the Golden Age upon Earth: *Love God and Love One Another.* Be *love in action.*

MIRACLES OF LOVE

Love Is The Key To Heal Humanity

There is no greater miracle than love to transform the ills of this world, to heal all dis-ease and imbalance within the mind, body and soul of humanity. Throughout history, sages and teachers of all spiritual pathways have written and spoken of the transformative power of love. More importantly, they have demonstrated love in action in their daily lives. This is the motto—and the goal—of all I Am Nation citizens.

Even the largest tome could not hold all the exquisite words that have been written on love, our divine birthright. The following are but a few key thoughts, intended to inspire.

THOUGHTS ON LOVE

Love the Lord your God with all your heart and with all your soul and with all your might and with all your mind. This is the greatest and the first commandment. And the second is like to it, Love your neighbor as yourself. On these two commandments hang the law and the prophets. . . .

This is my commandment, that you love one another as I have loved you. No one has greater love than this, to lay down one's life for one's friends. . . .

You have heard that it was said, "You shall love your neighbor and hate your enemy." But I say to you, Love your enemies and pray for those who persecute you, so that you may be children of your Father in heaven; for He makes His sun rise on the evil and on the good, and sends rain on the righteous and on the unrighteous.

For if you love those who love you, what reward do you have? Do not even the tax collectors do the same? And if you greet only your brothers and sisters, what more are you doing than others?

21

Do not even the Gentiles do the same? Be perfect, therefore, as your heavenly Father is perfect.

— Christ Jesus

•

You shall not hate your brother in your heart. . . . You shall not bear any enmity against the children of your own people, but you shall love your neighbor as yourself.

— Moses

•

In a Mahayana Buddhist text . . . Shantideva asks, "If you do not practice compassion toward your enemy then toward whom can you practice it?" . . . It is very important to develop the right attitude toward your enemy. If you can cultivate the right attitude, your enemies are your best spiritual teachers because their presence provides you with the opportunity to enhance and develop tolerance, patience, and understanding. By developing greater tolerance and patience, it will be easier for you to develop your capacity for compassion and, through that, altruism. So even for the practice of your own spiritual path, the presence of an enemy is crucial.

— Dalai Lama

•

He, who cannot forgive a trespass of malice to his enemy, has never yet tasted the most sublime enjoyment of love.

— Johann Kaspar Lavater

•

This supreme Lord who pervades all existence, the true Self of all creatures, may be realized through undivided love.

— Bhagavad Gita

•

Just as a mother would protect her only child at the risk of her own life, even so, cultivate a boundless heart towards all beings. Let your thoughts of boundless love pervade the whole world.

— Gautama Buddha

If I speak in the tongues of mortals and of angels, but do not have love, I am a noisy gong or a clanging cymbal. And if I have prophetic powers, and understand all mysteries and all knowledge, and if I have all faith, so as to remove mountains, but do not have love, I am nothing. If I give away all my possessions, and if I hand over my body so that I may boast, but do not have love, I gain nothing.

Love is patient; love is kind; love is not envious or boastful or arrogant or rude. It does not insist on its own way; it is not irritable or resentful; it does not rejoice in wrongdoing, but rejoices in the truth. It bears all things, believes all things, hopes all things, endures all things.

Love never ends. But as for prophecies, they will come to an end; as for tongues, they will cease; as for knowledge, it will come to an end. For we know only in part, and we prophesy only in part; but when the complete comes, the partial will come to an end.

When I was a child, I spoke like a child, I thought like a child, I reasoned like a child; when I became an adult, I put an end to childish ways. For now we see in a mirror, dimly, but then we will see face to face. Now I know only in part; then I will know fully, even as I have been fully known. And now faith, hope, and love abide, these three; and the greatest of these is love.

— Paul the Apostle

•

There is no fear in love, but perfect love casts out fear.

— Apostle John

•

Only love can bring individual beings to their perfect completion, as individuals, by uniting them one with another, because only love takes possession of them and unites them by what lies deepest within them.

— Pierre Teilhard de Chardin

•

Because of want of mutual love, all the calamities, usurpations, hatred, and animosity in the world have arisen. Therefore the man of humanity condemns it. . . . It should be replaced by the way of universal love and mutual benefit. . . . Those who love others will be loved by others. Those who benefit others will be benefited by others.

— Mo Tzu

•

Love oftentimes knoweth no measure, but is fervent beyond all measure. Love feels no burden, thinks nothing of trouble, attempts what is above its strength, pleads no excuse of impossibility; for it thinks all things lawful for itself and all things possible. It is therefore able to undertake all things; and it completes many things, and warrants them to take effect, where he who does not love would faint and lie down.

— Thomas à Kempis

•

To be in subjection to the higher Power is the highest goal of human attainment. The spirit of obedience is the spirit of love. Love is the most obedient thing in the universe.

CHARLES FILLMORE
Cofounder, with wife Myrtle, of Unity School of Christianity

Divine love is the force that dissolves all the opposers of true thought and thus smooths out every obstacle that presents itself. . . .

When the substance of divine love is poured out upon all alien thoughts we are not bothered by them anymore. This leads to joy, a positive force that has not been bearing fruit because of the obstructions heaped upon it by the failure to fulfill the law of the All-Good.

Love . . . is the feeling that excites desire for the welfare of its object. Unselfish love is fearless, because of its forgetfulness of self.

— Charles Fillmore

When the harshness of others seems to crush you, you can send forth love, the power that not only blesses you but goes forth to redeem the adverse conditions in the outer. When petals of the fragrant rose are crushed by cruel hands, they send forth their sweetness even more than before.

Forgiveness is the act of putting something else in the place of the thing forgiven. You put the positive realization of the Truth of Being in place of the appearance of negation and adversity which your senses and your intellectual training report. It does not matter that there is no immediate transformation; you have made use of your God-power to erase the appearance and to establish Truth. Such an attitude invites only the best from other souls.

Love that fulfills the law is the great sense of unity that prompts the soul to seek the understanding and practice of that which is for the welfare not only of the beloved but of all humanity.

— Myrtle Fillmore

•

It is my firm belief that it is love that sustains the Earth. There only is life where there is love. Life without love is death.

— Mahatma Gandhi

•

The supreme work to which we need to address ourselves in this world [is] to learn love. Is life not full of opportunities for learning love? Every man and woman every day has a thousand of them. The world is not a playground; it is a schoolroom. Life is not a holiday, but an education. The one eternal lesson for us all is how better we can love.

What makes a man a good cricketer? Practice. What makes a man a good artist, a good sculptor, a good musician? Practice. What makes a man a good linguist, a good stenographer? Practice. What makes a man a good man? Practice. Nothing else. . . .

Love is not a thing of enthusiastic emotion. It is a rich, strong . . . expression of the whole . . . Christlike nature in its fullest development. The constituents of this great character are only to be built up by ceaseless practice.

— Henry Drummond

25

To love, we must die continually to our own ideas, our own susceptibilities and our own comfort. The path of love is woven of sacrifice.

Stop looking for peace, give yourselves where you are. Stop looking at yourselves—look instead at your brothers and sisters in need. Be close to those God has given you in community today; work with the references which God has given you today. Ask how you can better love your brothers and sisters. Then you will find peace.

—Jean Vanier

•

Love is no deeper or more genuine than our willingness to suffer for the one loved. As Saint Teresa put it, "The measure of our love is the measure of the cross we can bear." . . .

It is a pity that so many people in the world confuse love, which is a spiritual thing, with attraction and pleasurable sensations, which are physical things. . . .

So many confuse pleasure with joy. Pleasure gratifies the senses. Joy is in the quiet of our will and is profoundly spiritual. Joy is deeper, surer, nobler, and more constant. And here is the wonder of joy: it can coexist with physical suffering, with privation, anguish, and even spiritual desolation. . . . It is the fruit of real love.

— Mother Catherine Thomas

•

Love is giving with no thought of getting. It is tenderness enfolding with strength to protect. It is forgiveness without further thought of the thing forgiven. It is understanding of the thing forgiven. It is understanding of human weakness, with knowledge of the true [person] shining through. It is quiet in the midst of turmoil. It is trust in God with no thought of self. It is the one altogether lovely, the light in the mother's eyes, the glory in the sacrifice, the quiet assurance of protection.

It is in the expectation of our Father's promise coming true. It is the refusal to see anything but good in our fellowman. It is the glory that comes with selflessness and the power that comes with assurance of the Father's love for His children. It is the voice that says "no" to our brother, though "yes" might be more easily said. It is

26

resistance to the world's lust and greed, thus becoming a positive law of annihilation to error.

Love: the one thing no one can take from us . . . the one thing we can give constantly and become increasingly rich in the giving. Love can take no offense, for it cannot know that which it does not of itself conceive. It cannot hurt or be hurt, for it is the purest reflection of God. Good. It is the one eternal, indestructible force for Good. It is the will of God, preparing, planning, proposing always what is best of all His universe.

– Author Unknown

CHANNELINGS ON LOVE

These interdimensional communications were channeled through me by ascended masters and archangels of the spiritual Hierarchy.

It is easy to love when you are loved, but difficult to love when you are hated or misused or ignored. This temptation [being unkind when unkindness is shown to you] is the easiest one to which to submit. Those who appear to you in unkindness, inconsideration, boorishness, lack of understanding are your tempters. If you can accept them as God's children and love them in return for their ill will and their hatred, then you can face the world as one of enlightenment. Every step of the disciple's path is fraught with this particular temptation, for you are never universally loved, understood or accepted.

– Sananda/Jesus; April 16, 1958

Attunement is not enough; action with love is attunement with Self. . . . You may step out of the physical into the high Self activity every time love speaks through action. Love of Self causes intunement, but love of God and man is action. . . . This is the New Age teaching. . . . So, New Age is action with high Self, action with love.

– Sananda/Jesus; July 7, 1960

Many you would designate Christ forces, or forces of light and of the understanding, are not of that light and not of that understanding; for they cannot accept fully, or cannot submit their individual wills to, the divine will for all mankind to share equally in the com-

27

ing Golden Era. These are not Christ-light brothers; only those are who can see all men equal, all men sharing fully what is to be, in substance and in knowledge, for their own sakes and for the sake of the whole race together expressing an individualization of the almighty, ever-living and ever-present God. . . .

This is one way of designating in your own consciousness who is of Christ force and who is of the anti-Christ force. You will see many, who will cry out that there is no God, come and fight shoulder to shoulder with you for peace and love and brotherhood equally for all men for all time. This is truly one who is of the Christ force. Yet you will have others, who profess to be of God, speaking words of God, who will say that some are to be saved and some are to be damned. These you will know are not of the Christ light; for the Christ light speaks of brotherhood first and foremost and will defend the right of all men everywhere to share equally with their brothers.

– Dr. Hannibal; August 9, 1961

Be that love force and use that love force in every conceivable situation. You have this power and will in you at all times. It is a matter of using it at will.

If you will, use love as divinely guided and directed in whatever measure you deem appropriate; but use it. If you cannot love a person or situation as it is, love that person and situation as it is meant to be or as you desire it to become. All is in a state of becoming. Therefore, what is the highest and greatest or most desirable activity, but love? So, become love in action. That is your scheme and your activity of future projects.

I ask and seek this in my name. For as I return unto the force field of Earth over a period of short years, I can only return through love and by the love power invoked for me and my mission concerning Earth.

Those who cannot love me by name must transmute these feelings of negativity, and love me for the works or desires of upliftment for the race which are done in my name. This is an example of the right use of the power of love. For to love and to bring love energy into any human situation is to equalize it with the Father-Mother Creative Principle. The equalizing both balances negativity into

positive response and causes a
new form to become manifested
in and through the person or conditions experiencing this particular vibration. . . .

You are not to be concerned
with doing this, as you do not do
anything. The law or Lord God
does all things. You are the focal
points of energy and creation
through which He works.

Therefore, make yourselves
agreeable and available for Him
to do this work. You do this by
becoming love in action. By
bringing love into focus and demonstration throughout the Earth
and in all parts of Earth form—
and this is the secret, the key, the
need—the time comes for this

SANANDA/JESUS
Prince of Love

energy pattern to materialize on Earth. For as you create this for-
mula for me and my works and my mission you create a new
heaven on a new Earth, and all will be made new and all men will
be able to renew that which has been outlived, as far as experience
and lessons here on Earth are concerned.

— Sananda/Jesus; October 20, 1969

Love is the key. It is the deciding factor which changes the blood-
stream, the chemistry, the energy form of your entire makeup physically, and then works forward into the light to meet its Self-equaliz-
ing incoming Source. This is the point in you where you become
transformed and will perform more clearly the works of God; as
you are gods in the making. We cannot emphasize this point more
forcefully into your conscious minds.

— Sananda/Jesus; October 21, 1969

As you learn more and more about your own light form, you
bring it into closer proximity to the Earth plane where you are

manifesting and exercising your spiritual rights, roles and privileges. This has a dire effect upon those in your immediate environment and circle. Those who are prepared and who have devoted themselves, dedicated themselves to this glory and eventual circumstance are delighted. They work with the changes, seek these changes in themselves and all around them, wish only for it to occur.

However, those unprepared, uninitiated, unaware are going to fight off the effect you have on them. They are going to alert all situations in their command to fight against what you symbolize and represent, not because they themselves are negative or ungodly but because they simply do not understand. You understand this, therefore you are required to be more tolerant, more patient and more loving than ever before.

This is why we have given you the important key immediately prior to this: love is the key. Through love you will divert negative forces and activities, even thought-energy patterns, from affecting your work, your lives and your organizational responsibilities. I must emphasize all this most strongly. . . . How else can I say it except: love is the key? Work in love with the light of your understanding, through all the truth, divine law principles. Never deviate one iota from this, otherwise you will invite consequences you will not be able to handle and from which we can do nothing, absolutely nothing, to save you.

– Sananda/Jesus; October 22, 1969

You must share, and share alike. You must be responsible for and love all equally to that which you love most dearly in yourself. What is it that man, or any life form, loves most dearly within himself, but the Life Source Itself? Living, thinking, feeling: this is life and energy, or God within you, expressing outwardly, that you love, that you cherish, and that you must love and cherish in all other things as much as you do in yourself. When you can share this equally and care about it equally for all other forms of life as you care about it for yourself, you will rehabilitate all other forms of life.

– Archangel Chamuel; October 26, 1971

KARMA
& REINCARNATION

In the beginning we were created as a spark or a light of God, His/Her children. This is a fact of life. All individuals—or spiritual, I Am Selves—are as cells in the one body which is called the Son of God; or, in Christianity, the body of Christ.

As man stepped down into matter to learn, to have experience, to share in the works of the Father-Mother God, he caused certain things to be put into motion which would bring about pertinent effects. *As you sow, so shall you reap.* This is the law of karma—an ancient Sanskrit term—which is an impersonal, changeless cosmic principle that is continuously in effect and which results in the balancing of good and bad thoughts and deeds. An understanding of this law will free the human mind from harboring resentment against God or man, for it is a law of equalization, a fact of life, that man cannot change.

Since it is impossible to learn or to equalize everything in one life span or one period of time or one dimension or one set of circumstances, the spirit or the I Am Self, working through the soul, which is the accumulation of all lessons and experiences, creates new bodies and new situations. This enables us to reembody in an area of learning and to continue studying our relationship with God. This is known as reincarnation.

&

KARMA

Definition:
Debit and credit system based on the law of cause and effect

Picture in your mind a scale of justice. See truth and perfection on one side and mortal error on the other. We work constantly for the outcome of our thoughts and deeds to be on the right or the truth side. Our I Am or Christ Selves constantly guide us to experience the lessons that will enhance our spiritual growth. We are continually impressed to make the right choice in all situations that arise. With each successful overcoming we lighten our personal karmic obligations, which in turn lightens the karma of the masses.

Mankind has insisted too much on learning by stress, by experiencing the agonies and the ecstasies. Since the days of Lemuria and Atlantis man has evolved in an upward trend through the dark ages of spiritual ignorance, during which time lessons have been learned that are wholly valuable to the present era of time known as the Mark Age (age of marks and signs of the ending of the ages of materiality and the beginning of the age of spirituality).

That is why humanity now is more capable and ready to go into the Golden Age than back in the Atlantean days. The masses have suffered the elimination of much karma and are having the opportunity presented to them once more to be truly free.

TYPES OF KARMA

There are various types of karma that we deal with in our lifetime. Each of us has contact with many varieties to one degree or another. There are debits and credits that are brought into this life from previous lifetimes on this sphere and elsewhere. There is inevitable karma we take upon ourselves by the mere act of incarnating upon the Earth, for there are family, group, national and planetary karmas which we inherit by association. We also face new karma, both good and bad, brought about by the use of our own free will during our present lifetime.

32

Personal karma we bring into this life with us is possibly the most misunderstood. You hear of good-living people who seem to suffer one terrible thing after another. There also seem to be many individuals who in selfish inconsideration constantly harm others and appear to get away with it. Payment, or karmic equalization, does not come always at the time of the act, but always will come when the impact is great enough to implant firmly the lesson to be learned.

This can be immediate or can carry over into a future lifetime. When there is no apparent cause for hardship in this life, you can be assured that the hardship was earned in a previous incarnation. By the same token, those who harm others and go unchallenged will have to deal with the consequences when it is most timely.

Often you will see family groups equalizing previous-life karmic debts, as in the case of a couple desperately wanting a child and going fruitless, or having a crippled child. It is asked how an innocent child who did no wrong has earned such trials. How do we not know this soul was not guilty of crippling others in a former incarnation? The karma of the parents could figure in, such as their not wanting children or having abused children in past life experiences.

The lesson earned will be strong enough for the soul to remember and to take on as a part of himself when he learns he is not punished *for* his sins, as is the popular misconception, but that he is punished *by* his sins.

Mass, group and national karma are met and equalized in the same manner as individual karma. Often many souls will make the transition, or will leave the Earth plane, at the same time, such as in airplane crashes or battles of war, which in turn also involves the relatives who still are living. It is possible these groups of souls may have been involved in a group karmic debt. Mass exterminations are such possibilities. The I Am Self of each soul selects the time and circumstances for erasing the karmic debt that will prove most fruitful and thereby will allow further progression.

PLANETARY KARMA

The race of man on Earth has accrued karma as the laggards of this solar system. They contribute to this by refusing to live in a

33

spiritual or Christlike manner. When incarnating into the Earth plane, we take upon ourselves, or share a part of, this existing karma. Mass karma is an invisible load which each of us as light workers is bound to help find ways to eliminate or to lighten through our love and service.

The devic or nature forces which form the physical structure of the planet also react to man's thinking and actions, be they erroneous or of truth. The inharmony of man affects the nature forces, which mirror the thoughts and deeds of man. When these forces are overloaded with inharmony they sometimes react in environmental disturbances which are cataclysmic. This purging or Earth cleansing does much toward equalizing some of the mass karma. With right thinking, mankind could bring about this cleansing in an easier fashion, thereby sparing much needless suffering.

Between incarnations there is Earth karma being worked out on the astral planes surrounding and interpenetrating the Earth. There also is karma being worked out by other kingdoms on Earth, such as the animal kingdom. This is the last opportunity for all kingdoms on Earth to be prepared for graduation to the next higher dimension, as this period ends by divine decree on or about the turn of the twenty-first century.

NOT ALL BAD

Karma we assume willingly or of our own free will means that which we agree to pay as the price for an action or a deed we choose to perform. Good or bad, with free will we take on new karma in each life. We reap what we sow. This is a fact of life.

Good karma is earned as well as bad karma. We might well have an abundance of good karma accrued that is helping us in many ways during the present lifetime. It can be likened unto a savings account from which we can draw. There are many persons going through life with one good thing after another being given to them.

Good karma which one has to his credit does not have to be repaid as the same deeds one has performed, but will manifest in at least the same or greater consideration or proportion. Good karma is never destroyed, for it stands in the personal record. Error karma is transmutable and eventually is neutralized.

There is no karma attached to the elimination of parasites, for these feed on other life forms. This is against the law, the law of God or the law of Energy. Parasites have been created by mankind's error thinking; therefore, we must strive to eliminate them in this Latter-Day period of cleansing and transmutation.

HOW TO HANDLE KARMA

The best and most practical way to deal with undesirable karma is by dedication to Spirit's works. Doing any job that comes to you to do, regardless of how menial it may seem, when performed with love and sincere application and with no thought of reward or compliment is a sure way to help cleanse a karmic record. If you had been committing error deeds in this lifetime before gaining some illumination and understanding as to what you had been doing, it still would be possible to eliminate some or all of the debt by the doing of good works for Spirit.

This depends, of course, on the extent or degree of the bad deeds. A good example of a spiritual turnabout was demonstrated by Saul who, upon seeing the folly of his actions, devoted the balance of his life as Paul the Apostle to Spirit's cause. He created his pattern on Earth so none who came afterward could deny the possibility of grace through change and right action.

At this time in our solar system's development, the Earth is an ideal place to clear up past karmic obligations. This special Mark Age period of time, in which cleansing and transmutation are being expressed, has attracted many souls here for this very purpose. The higher vibrations of the approaching Golden Age of Aquarius aid all of us to do the right thing with less resistance, thereby overcoming old problems and lightening our negative karma.

Individually we also can help others to erase some of their karma by forgiving them their trespassing against us. Forgiving is a way of working with higher understanding and is important for all to practice.

Sometimes spiritual masters will take upon themselves a portion of karma to help in individual or mass cleansing here in the physical or Earth plane. This was most aptly demonstrated by Jesus of Nazareth through his exampling. It was not necessary for Jesus to go through his suffering because of his own karma. Rather, in the plan of Spirit, he chose to example for the benefit of all humankind.

ASTROLOGY

A soul may incarnate on a certain day, hour and place when the celestial rays are in mathematical harmony with his/her individual karma. A horoscope chart is a personal portrait possibly indicating one's prior development and showing potential opportunities for erasing negative karma or for utilizing good karma, and for passing old tests and learning new lessons. We are not bound by our fate. We created it and we can change it. It can be overcome by our spiritual resources, which are *not* controlled by planetary influences.

THE GOAL

How do we avoid making karma of the wrong kind? It is in elimination of the mortal ego that the soul can be free to live and to act in a selfless and unattached manner of service, thereby incurring no negative karma. Thus we achieve the ultimate goal of true freedom and oneness with our high or I Am Self. This is the destiny for man in the Golden Era now dawning upon the face of the Earth, when Earthman shall be free from bondage and shall regain his natural heritage as a true child of our Father-Mother God.

REINCARNATION

Definition:

**Reembodying on a plane or planet
where the soul has had previous incarnation**

Karma is the divine law of cause and effect. One purpose of reincarnation is to pay off negative karma or debts that have been caused in prior lives. Some become linked to the wheel of reincarnation and karma, thereby shuttling back and forth between the physical and astral realms until all nonspiritual desires are completely worked out and fulfilled regarding Earth attachments. The major effort of the program for mankind during this transitional, forty-year Mark Age period (approximately 1960–2000) is to accomplish this and to evolve beyond it.

SCHOOLROOM OF EARTH

Let us liken the Earth unto a schoolroom; or unto a taskmaster, and an exacting one at that. For we each have come here to learn many lessons for our own soul evolvement and to contribute to the race of man that which we have learned from our individual past experiences. There are many who have been here many times, or in similar areas in various parts of the galaxy.

We not only incarnate on the Earth plane but also in the astral planes around and interpenetrating the Earth. Thereby we work in and through those areas, to and for the Earth. As on the physical, the astral planes have many lessons to teach us and many individual desires to be fulfilled. Many there also need help and guidance.

During our soul evolvement on Earth we have been in many circumstances at one time or another. It is not possible to experience every lesson in one incarnation, due to the variety of possible life expressions. We have been both male and female. We have taken on incarnation in various races, creeds and geographical areas. We have lived under many conditions and circumstances, perhaps as kings or slaves, as masters or students.

In each lifetime we developed a personality based on prior lives and the current one. It is through this wonderful variety of life expressions that we grow in soul evolution, profiting from the experiences and the lessons in this schoolroom of life.

After a soul has had a number of incarnations on Earth, as both male and female and in various situations, and has succeeded in gaining a certain degree of balance or mastership over his or her actions on the Earth plane, he/she could be allowed to reincarnate so as to enhance certain talents and powers, or so as to help others. So-called natural talents likely are those mastered in prior lives. This is especially demonstrated in the arts, such as painting and music. The naturalness of performance is due to having developed such in previous lives.

It is when we are accomplished in a field that we can be used as a valuable, clear and open channel for Spirit to project energies through for the benefit of mankind. It is this unobstructed openness that causes others to pay special attention to an artist. We can appreciate an exceptional artist because of our own inherent ability to detect an open and clear channel.

It is not necessary for each soul to experience personally every possible life expression. There are many things that can be satisfied vicariously through understanding of or association with another's fulfillment. For example, one may be married to a painter and thereby partially live the life of a painter. In this close relationship one could either satisfy the desire for this manifestation or utilize this incarnation as a grounding for further application in this field in the future.

FAILING A LESSON

Most of us have experienced failures in learning lessons. Sometimes we are aware of such failures and seek to rectify error thinking so as to overcome our shortcomings. In other cases it may require more severe methods, even may need additional incarnations to balance out and to learn.

Learning the responsibility and the proper usage of money as a spiritual tool is a good example. Money is symbolic of spiritual energy supply. One who is given wealth but who becomes selfish or miserly or hurts others through the misuse of that wealth fails to understand his obligation. If he fails to see his folly during one life span, he has created karma on the debit side of the ledger and later must reap what he has sown. A future lifetime could find him frustrated due to lack of money. This is not God's revenge, but a tax placed upon him by his own high Self. Through these trials the soul learns to temper values properly and thereby grow accordingly.

PAST-LIFE RECALL

Some people have strong memory recall of past-life experiences brought about by dreams or visions, by visiting an area for the first time and finding familiar subconscious memories stirring, and just by knowing. There are others who actively seek information of their own past lives from those who are psychic or are channels for information. But, a word of caution: in many cases this sort of alleged channeling can be fraught with error, although certainly not always.

If necessary or beneficial to the soul's development, it could be given by one's Christ Self, even if not in precise and explicit words, if it would add to better understanding of the present life expression. For example, if it would be revealed that you were a doctor previously, this could confirm why you are seeking to study some aspect of the medical field in this lifetime, and would help you proceed with the strength of your convictions that you were doing the right thing.

We may have had many good and satisfying incarnations previously that are totally irrelevant to our function at the present time in that they have no direct applicable value. On the other hand, this knowledge possibly could make our mortal ego swell to a point of slowing down current development. It should be understood that each soul is the product of a vast number of life experiences in many areas of the solar system.

The current incarnation is important as a result of all the lifetimes that have gone before and as a prelude to the ones to follow. We have passed through all the others to arrive at the current step in our climb towards perfection. What we do in this one during this critical turning point in evolution (the Mark Age period or the Latter Days) may set the course for millions of our incarnations ahead.

Not having conscious recall of previous lives is a blessing for most on Earth now. In the case of being here to learn a lesson we may have failed previously, a premature knowledge of this failure could set into motion old subconscious fear patterns that could cause us to fail again. In between Earth incarnations we have been reinforced with lessons and new understandings to help us rise above our failings. With a fresh start and approach, we can attack what may have been a persistent problem and can succeed in mastering it.

Therefore, it often is better not to know of previous experiences until we have grown in understanding and awareness so as to be able to cope more easily with them and thereby benefit from these revelations. The entire race of man on Earth in time will reach a point when all will have conscious recall of past incarnations. We each will have access to our akashic or soul record and will gain the benefit of previous experiences of our varied life expressions.

TYPICAL SOUL PROBLEMS

Many are working out problems brought forth from previous lifetimes without being aware of the problems' origins. For example, fear of drowning or of fire or of height could have been brought about by having a previous lifetime end through going down in a ship, being trapped in a fire or falling from a high place. Conflict with an individual for no apparent reason could be a continuation of or the result of a previous-lifetime encounter. Some cannot tolerate extreme climates, which is understandable if they previously had frozen to death or had died from desert heat. A prejudice could be an unresolved karmic debt.

Most of these types of problems are overcome gradually with normal growth development. If we are persistent we can be shown in a dream sequence or in meditation a flashback of the scene of the cause. This gives understanding and enough insight to overcome unfounded present fears and allows us to grow without those encumbrances.

BETWEEN EARTH INCARNATIONS

The period of rest required for each soul between incarnations is variable and is determined by many factors. Sometimes it is governed by the manner of the soul's exit from this plane. A peaceful transition would aid a soul to easier adjustment in its next step of progress, whereas a shocking lifetime with a violent death could be very traumatic. The soul then would require a longer period of rest for healing and balance before it could gain the necessary strength and courage to cope with those things which would be required of it during the next incarnation.

Sometimes a longer period of time between incarnations might be necessary because a particular opportunity on Earth or elsewhere would have passed. Therefore, that soul would have to wait until the right circumstances once again were presented through environmental or evolutionary changes so as to allow a given lesson or function to be enacted. We all are here at any given time because it is ideal or best suited for us to learn important lessons and because we have valuable services to render unto Spirit and our fellowman.

There is no truth to various theories that there always is a set or determinable length of time between incarnations, or that there is a universal pattern which establishes the sex.

CHOOSING A VEHICLE

Is there a choice on the other side in selecting where, when and how we will incarnate for our next life on Earth? This is primarily a matter of evolution and availability, as to what choices the soul is allowed. A soul that still is seeking to master the basic lessons of this physical plane would have less choice than a more Earthly experienced or more highly evolved soul who is a worker for the spiritual program, which is guided by the ascended masters on the etheric and the archangels who comprise the spiritual government or Hierarchal Board of our solar system.

Such a program worker could choose his parents from those who are readying physical vehicles at the time best suited for him to incarnate and to bring forth his function on the physical plane. The choice is made from the I Am Self state of consciousness rather than from the mortal state. If a life of hardship rather than luxury would better allow the soul to accomplish its goal, that is the one that would be selected. For the enlightened worker, serving the spiritual, evolutionary program is above all other desires.

There may be a latitude of time permitted a soul to take over final possession of a new physical vehicle or body. The soul takes over at the time of birth in a gradual manner, sometimes taking many months for full control. An eager soul taking partial residence may want to experience and to oversee each stage of physical development. Another may go in and out of the newly born body many times so as to adjust to the body and environment. There may be a visible change in a newborn child, a new spark to its being, when the soul finally takes permanent residence.

41

I AM SELF IN CONTROL OF VEHICLE

Our I Am Selves attempt to guide us at all times and in all planes of existence. Sometimes a soul will have a so-called abnormal or overly strong desire that will override the high Self's direction. He or she might seek an incarnation for self-gratification and accomplish little or no spiritual development.

In this case the high Self permits the soul to incarnate into a life stream where this desire can be fulfilled and get it out of his or her system. Of course, Spirit does step in to the point where the proper lesson can be presented. Along with self-gratification there possibly could be great hardship on one level or another to neutralize or to offset the desire and the temporary sidetracking from the spiritual goal.

CLEARING MISCONCEPTIONS

Many people labor under the erroneous impression that reincarnation means we can come back to Earth such as an animal, a bird, an insect or a tree. This is the transmigration theory and is completely false. Another totally false concept is that humanity has reached its present state of being by evolving from a one-cell organism upwards through the various classes of life forms until it finally reaches man or human status.

Each species of life form was placed upon the Earth in its own kingdom. Each lower kingdom has its own evolvement and development separate and distinct from the race of man, the Son of God, in this third dimensional plane of Earth. This is so stated in the Holy Bible and can be found clearly outlined in the first chapter of the book of Genesis.

There still will be those who will ask: but how do we know there is such a thing as reincarnation; who has told us so? Many spiritual leaders and teachers have stated so. The verification for one's own acceptance comes through one's own Self from within. As we rise in evolvement we accept revelations given to us either by our high Selves or by intunements of others who are clear channels.

We must become receptive to the idea before information and understanding on reincarnation can be accepted and of benefit. We must accept the concept of reincarnation before we can get into higher concepts, as this is a basic premise for other soul-satisfying truths.

PERFECT EXAMPLE

The prime and highest examples of reincarnation on Earth have been demonstrated by Sananda, our spiritual leader and the Prince of the planet Earth. He was an avatar who came onto Earth often when mankind was in need of light or was ready for higher teachings. He incarnated in many of the major philosophies and religions so as to bring forth light and spiritual growth. Among other incarnations, he was the biblical Moses of the Hebrews, Gautama Buddha of the Orientals, Socrates for the Greeks and the philosophers and the intellectuals. His last incarnation on Earth was the most perfect example, as Jesus of Nazareth. (See also the Glossary.)

He will return again around the turn of the twenty-first century to take up his role as the spiritual leader of Earth. Once more he will lead mankind into the next step of spiritual development and evolvement. He is the way shower for each of us to identify with and to understand why it has been necessary for most on Earth to come back often, or to avail ourselves of reincarnation as a spiritual aid for evolution.

There are many passages in the Holy Bible referring to reincarnation, although it was attempted to have all such removed. But this fact of life is so interwoven that it could not be denied entirely. About five hundred years after the compilation of many Hebraic and Christian scriptures, there were many statements deleted in the preparation of our present Holy Bible. Some of this was to keep certain information secret and some was through error and lack of spiritual understanding.

One deleted scripture is what now is called the long-lost *Second Book of Acts.* It is devoted to some of the prior incarnations of Mary and Jesus. It explains in simple detail some lessons learned through their concurrent or at-the-same-time incarnations. These revealing discourses were spoken by Mary to the disciples as she prepared for her transition at the age of eighty-three.

This book, truly a must for all truth seekers, is available through Mark-Age, retitled as *Seven Lives of Mary & Jesus* ($5). It was published originally in 1904 by the scholarly Dr. Kenneth Sylvan Guthrie and was on file in the Library of Congress, where Mark-Age obtained a copy and brought it into the light once more.

EARTH GRADUATION

After our souls have learned sufficient lessons and have evolved enough on Earth to go into higher realms for further development, we can volunteer to incarnate again on Earth in order to help raise our brothers and sisters to a higher level of understanding. This is the ultimate sacrifice and the true meaning of, "No one has greater love than this, to lay down one's life for one's friends."

A prime example of this was Sananda's last incarnation on Earth as Jesus of Nazareth, where the soul already was so cleansed and purified that a virgin birth was possible. Every act in that incarnation was a demonstration for all men to emulate. It was not that he *died* for his fellowmen but that he showed us how really to *live*.

Ultimately man will see and will demonstrate that there is no death. We will transmute and will raise the vibration of the physical body into the etheric or light body and will take it with us when we have finished our work here. Those on higher realms by merely raising or lowering their vibrational level are able to manifest a vehicle or a body on any plane or dimension they have mastered. Eventually we all will be able to go into and to come out of any realm we desire to visit, in this same manner.

Man on Earth is being aided by highly evolved souls from all over the solar system, and beyond, who are taking up incarnation on Earth to bring their special functions and vibrations to aid and to enhance the evolvement of the planet. Earth is behind the other planets in our solar system in spiritual development. It is in great need of help at this time of cleansing and change, this long-prophesied Judgment Day. The light workers, which hopefully include all of us on Earth, literally are tuning up the Earth so it can join the solar system in a grand chorus of spiritual harmony. When this is accomplished, truly the lost chord will have been found.

For those who cannot accept yet the concepts of karma and reincarnation in their search for higher understanding, there may be good reasons for such resistance. Those concepts which seem difficult to accept should be set aside temporarily and not be discarded completely, for such ideas at a later time in the growth pattern may be found to be seeds which blossom into full bloom and beauty.

CHANNELINGS ON REINCARNATION

Of the numerous references to reincarnation channeled through me by the ascended masters, and published by Mark-Age since 1960, here are three.

"Man grows and slips back, grows and slips back; seldom is it all in one direction. That is why we have the law of reincarnation, so man can repeatedly return to learn his lessons. When he learns a lesson he cannot unlearn it. It goes with him and he uses it, and thereby strengthens it by that use. He comes to learn certain other lessons which have been difficult for him. By practicing, suffering, living he is taught and strengthened to grow in new directions, to overcome old, bad, useless habits."

— Paul the Apostle; March 25, 1958

"It was never Spirit's will not to teach reincarnation. It is in the teachings. In no religion or in no teachings could it be entirely removed. . . . Always, somehow, somewhere a small seed or spark is left. This is true in Christian and Judaic teachings today. Reincarnation is there, but only in a very small segment of truth. They could not remove it entirely, though many have tried."

— Sananda/Jesus; October 4, 1960

"We have experiences on other planes and planets besides Earth focal point. The Earth focal point refers not only to a physical expression as you understand it, of life after life on Earth–which many understand as reincarnation–but it refers to your evolvement on other inner planes, higher planes where you are not confined to a physical body but express in a higher, more refined manner using mostly mind powers and mind functions and faculties."

— Mary the Mother; January 9, 1963

COMMUNICATION VIA CHANNELING

Synonym:

Channel, Prophet, Seer, Medium, Sensitive

Definition:

A course into which something may be directed; a means of passage or transmission; a frequency range sufficient to transmit a single message

HISTORY

The art of channeling is not new to the Earth. It only has changed names, depending on the civilization or the evolutionary period in which various teachers have expressed spiritual understanding and spiritual information to help mankind.

Also, it has changed in its level of acceptance. In many societies, the high priests and priestesses were looked upon as gods who could mediate between worlds. Often they fulfilled great functions, but many corrupted their talent and misused their power over the masses.

Thus, in our present materialistic society, channels or those with psychic power often have been suspect, held in disrepute and mistrusted. But because we are in the Latter Days or the Mark Age, it must be put back into its proper perspective as a spiritual gift or talent and as a true heritage of our Sonship with the Father-Mother God, our Creator. At the same time, we must now correlate it to our present-day, advanced knowledge of mental and physical sciences. Channeling must no longer be a mysterious, hidden or occult art.

Great books and teachings such as the Holy Bible and other scriptures actually are channeled communications or inspired messages received either from the I Am Self of the writer or spiritual consciousness of those on other planes or planets, relaying how man must live in this mortal realm according to Spirit's immutable divine laws and principles.

In these end times, all things that have been hidden are being brought to the surface for mankind to discern and to decide what is for his higher good and for the race's future usage. What is no longer applicable or needed for spiritual growth must be discarded in this Mark Age, purification period.

Mankind is evolving in this age to a new level of understanding and expression on the Earth. The planet, man and all life form on it are gradually moving into the fourth dimension. This will tear away the veils that prevent us from seeing and communicating with man of the other planes and planets in this solar system.

Communication via channeling will expand our understanding and information about all these other planes, the astral, etheric and celestial realms. By communicating with those beings on other planes and planets, we will receive the guidance and the help we need in these changing events.

The higher teachings from those on the etheric and the celestial or angelic realms give us the assistance we need to eliminate that which has been in error and to bring forth the spiritual laws into our present consciousness, bodies and environment.

By the time we have risen into the fourth dimensional plane of consciousness—which is to occur during the Aquarian Age, after the year 2000—man of Earth will be utilizing this function of communication via channeling much more than now. Telepathy is one of our inherent Christ abilities, a natural talent of our higher Self in action.

WHO IS A CHANNEL?

Every single person is a channel. Each of us expresses individualized Divine Energy in one form or another and on one level or another. Energy is expressed through various vibrations. Energy can be relayed on specific levels. Vibratory impulses can occur through sound, music, words, mental and physical images, and thoughts. In addition, specific vibratory rates can be felt, sensed, known and intuited.

We express our own individual frequency rate which is unique and unduplicated. But it is to be perfected, utilized, expressed and exchanged with others for complementary and supplementary purposes. Each is a part of the Divine, and all parts of Divine Energy are the sum total of the whole, which is God.

If we each are properly intuned and follow that inner impulse or guidance of our specific Divine Energy impulse, we receive our own distinct personal program and plan for existence at that particular time and place in our eternal ongoing through infinite specific experiences and incarnations.

As we all develop our consciousness or awareness of the Cosmic Force within, of which we are a part, we will come to recognize the multitudinous ways in which we are used as channels. Thereby we help to develop and to bring forth all that is inherent within us. In other words, we will learn our specific talents and functions, which are unique, specialized and individualized for each one's particular existence.

The I Am Nation via Mark-Age teaches that this inner guidance or spiritual communication comes from one's own higher Self, known as the Christ or I Am Self. Or, it may come from the etheric and the celestial guardians and teachers who work and cooperate with us and through us until we reach that communion (communication) with our own individualized immortal Self within.

Every individual on Earth or on any other plane of existence is perfectly capable of receiving directly, without any interference, from his I Am Self. With training and preparation we become capable of receiving or communicating with anyone else in the same dimension or from other dimensions. The advantage of this communication is to receive guidance and assistance for those roles, missions and lessons we need in our spiritual ongoing and unfoldment in the infinite, expanding cosmos.

One of our most profound lessons in evolutionary progress is our interrelationship and interdependence with each other and with the many other forms of Life Force. Through the communications via channeling, we learn many of these experiences, which are not always obvious to the mortal, sensual, third dimensional plane of existence.

TYPES OF CHANNELING

1. Trance or Sleep Mediumship. The person loses total conscious awareness and then speaks in this state, perhaps in languages unknown and about subjects unfamiliar to the present personality development.

This information can come either from his or her own subconscious memory bank, carried in the astral body which is the sum total of past incarnations; and/or from astral beings who control the body and the mind at that time, wherein the medium vacates his or her own vehicle and allows this takeover.

2. Automatic Writing, Drawing or Music. Forces from another level, from the subconscious memory, or from the superconscious, I Am Self take control over the hands and perform through them. The person is usually conscious or semiconscious and cooperates with the process, though not always understanding the material as it comes forth.

3. Clairaudience (clear hearing), Clairvoyance (clear seeing), Clairsentience (clear sensing or feeling). These are our spiritual senses, beyond the physical frequency range. Voices, visions, information channeled from the astral, etheric or celestial planes can be received without our conscious control or desire. They are spontaneous and independent experiences and are not the result of the person's training.

4. Mental Telepathy or Thought Transference. Specific words or ideas are projected through the brain apparatus of the conscious medium or channel, to be written or spoken. This usually occurs after having experienced some of the prior three, as it is much more complex and requires conscious training.

A highly developed channel can work cooperatively, but with complete objectivity and impersonalness, with a master of the etheric or with angelic beings of the celestial so that control over the physical mechanism is possible to the extent that exact words or inflections can be expressed.

This is the highest form of communication via channeling in the evolvement of man on Earth now. Such channels are on the road to complete Christ consciousness or mastery on the physical, for the process helps to transmute them in body, mind and soul.

5. Space Beams. Extraterrestrial spacecraft can use electromagnetic beams to transmit thoughts and words to, or physical control over, those on Earth. Usually this occurs with those interested in psychic and spiritual matters. But it also is occurring now to those with no prior training or understanding. This can be traumatic if not understood, and is one reason why information and education on these changing conditions in our world during this Mark Age period and program are so essential.

Space beams usually are felt physically, such as: a helmet or cap clamped on the top of the head, pressure across the forehead or at the temples, a rod or a beam from the head down through the spine, a sudden chill or heat which turns off as though by a switch and leaves no aftereffect or sensation. Healings have been known to occur in this manner.

6. Inspiration, Intuition or Hunches. Specific or general information can be relayed to the conscious mind either through the subconscious memory pattern (soul or past experiences), through the superconscious (the I Am or high Self within), or from those of other planes and planets.

This is the most common form of communication, which has manifested in all forms of art; in many scientific discoveries, inspirations and inventions; in abstract philosophies, religious theology and other teachings; and in guiding each one of us in our individual growth and understanding.

Many masters have incarnated throughout Earth history to implant new ideas and information to help build a bridge from mortal to immortal experience for the entire race. These masters are not usually aware of who they are or why they came. But they bring with them, and leave through their works, higher energy forms for the gradual upliftment and transmutation of Earth expression from the third dimensional (physical) into the fourth dimensional (spiritual) expression.

7. I Am Consciousness. Direct knowing and experiencing from the God Self within. The individual can communicate consciously with all energy forms in the universe, thus knowing and seeing that

51

all things are part of the All, which is the one and only God, who is Creative Energy in action.

CHANNELS TRANSMIT ENERGY

We each channel our own individualized vibratory rate of energy. We channel or transfer this energy consciously or unconsciously according to our evolvement, our understanding and our acceptance of this spiritual function. But it operates whether we accept it or not.

If we have understanding and acceptance we can project our own unique, special, individual energy to areas, persons or conditions which can be aided, inspired or healed. This is love (God) in action.

That which you sow you shall reap. Therefore, send out or project your spiritual energies. Channel the proper thoughts to those from whom you wish certain correct and proper (spiritual) effects or actions.

No matter what field of endeavor—business, farming, school, home, community affairs—you can and should channel ideas of good to others with whom you are associated. Through the law of cause and effect, what you feel, send, and desire returns unto you. *Be sure to send only good so that only good shall return to you.* This also is channeling.

NEED FOR CURRENT COMMUNICATIONS

The present age we are living in, from approximately 1960 to 2000, is called the Mark Age period and program, the time of signs or marks of the age. In scriptures this is known as the Latter Days, the cleansing period, the purification time. This interim, transition cycle is almost at an end.

As man has gone through this difficult period of his evolution on Earth, it has been necessary to receive current communications from the spiritual forces who govern and guide us in our evolutionary progress. Thus, many channels, prophets or sensitives purposely have incarnated on Earth in these Latter Days to relay to mankind what is needed for his immediate understanding and urgent actions in order to go through this forty-year cleansing and purification.

In the forthcoming spiritual cycle on Earth, the Golden Age of Aquarius, man is to experience the Second Coming. This refers both to the entire race as it experiences its second opportunity to express Christ or cosmic consciousness on the Earth, as before the fall of man into physical matter (see our textbook *Evolution of Man*), and also the Second Coming of the spiritual ruler of this planet.

This ruler, who last incarnated as Jesus of Nazareth, is known on the higher planes of existence as Sananda, one of the seven directors of the spiritual government or Hierarchal Board of our solar system. Each of Sananda/Jesus' lives or incarnations on Earth (see Glossary) guided mankind to another level of spiritual understanding, until in his last Earth life he demonstrated the resurrection or the light body of the I Am or Christ consciousness. "What I have done," he said, "you shall do; even greater things."

One of these greater things is for a minimum of one hundred and forty-four thousand in Christ consciousness and in their light or etheric bodies to help lift and transmute Earth and all forms upon it, including mankind, from the third dimensional frequency (physical matter) into the fourth dimensional frequency form (spiritual form or light body which Jesus demonstrated after his crucifixion).

This general theme and message now are being broadcast by many channels, prophets and sensitives on Earth. Some work within their own family. Others work in groups and in churches of all denominations. Still others are inspired to publish this material and to circulate it for many others to read, to study and to use.

When most of these channeled messages or inspirations are correlated, they reflect one important, common theme: Earthman is evolving into another dimension, is becoming Christed through his present Earth-body frequency, and this is resulting in a crucifixion of the old in order to prepare for the resurrection of the new.

Another great service, but one which is very subtle and is performed consciously or unconsciously by channels of light, is the mental broadcasting of this information, thus making it a part of the subconscious record of the entire race. These mental broadcasts individually and collectively create a thought form of spiritual energy which is subliminally absorbed through the subconscious minds of all persons. Each receives these energy impulses whether aware of them or not. They come in dreams, inspired thoughts, flashes of intuition or revelation, spoken or written words that suddenly ring true within and make sense to the conscious mind.

This is one of the services channels are performing in these end days. It is one of the signs or marks of this age when, as the Holy Bible says, "My spirit shall pour out upon all flesh."

CLEARING A CHANNEL

The projections and information from the etheric and celestial planes are true and clear when they are sent forth. However, when they pass through the subconscious, to be picked up by the conscious mind of the channel, they can be shaded, colored or distorted to various degrees.

The highest and safest form of receiving is via the superconscious or I Am Self of the channel. This is why Mark-Age emphasizes first, foremost and predominantly that everyone is obliged to develop, to refine and to evolve into his or her own Christed being. But regardless of whether an individual is in that I Am state or not, he or she is capable of receiving communications from others who are in that high estate.

It is erroneous to believe that when we reach the I Am state we lose or do not need communication from anyone or anything else. To the contrary; when in that state, we are in constant communion (communication) with all other life form, as part of the One and All that is. Remember, no one part of God can know or express all of God. We complement and supplement each other.

In the process of developing and reaching this I Am state of consciousness we must learn to discern what is clear, what might have been shaded and what might have been distorted in the natural channeling procedures.

Mental cleansing must occur first. One must release and transmute every thought of resentment, malice, criticism and confusion. This results in tremendous emotional and physical cleansings. Rigorous routines and changes are given to the dedicated channel that transmute the body, the mind and the soul of the individual over long periods of time, usually over a series of lifetimes.

Messages that are received during this period usually pertain to the individual's personal life, unfoldment and development. The messages during this training period generally should be applied to the channel and associates, not to the masses or the world at large.

A channel is cleared only after he or she has evolved to the point of needing or desiring no personal attention, gratification or acclaim due to that material for which he or she is responsible. This takes much discipline and examination by that individual and by those who are affected by the works of that one.

PROTECTION OF THE CHANNEL

When the channel opens to receive communication from the hidden realms, he immediately is vulnerable to all thoughts that are circulating within his plane of operation; in this case, the planet Earth. He also is susceptible to thoughts from the lower astral planes which are attracted to the light and the energy projected from his auric field. Therefore, it is absolutely essential for the channel to place himself in the protective light of his Christ body.

Visualize your higher Self or light body as a cocoon approximately two to four feet away from the physical and auric fields. Weave this light as a protective coat around the entire physical and auric fields, slowly and methodically spinning counterclockwise, until it reaches the top of your head. This is the crown or highest spiritual center, through which the Christ Self enters.

Do not close off your crown chakra. Leave it open to your I Am Self, which is an individualization of God. This is an opening or a stem which is your lifeline throughout eternity.

Never channel when there is any disturbance in the mind, the body or the emotions of yourself or of those with whom you are working in a group. This is extremely important, because the channel is open to receive all thoughts and emotions which are circulating from within himself and from those around him.

Usually in group activity there are one or more individuals who find that they act as batteries for the channel. These are individuals who use their spiritual energies or focus of light to enhance the receiving of thoughts and energies that pass through the one who acts as the channel. Their love and dedication protect the channel from disturbances and distortions.

This is an expression of positive and negative force fields or polarities. The channel is the negative polarity, the receiver. The battery is the positive polarity, the strengthener and the protector of the auric field through which the ideas and energies must penetrate in order for the channel to pick them up and to record them.

VERIFICATION IS ESSENTIAL

Every sincere channel who truly wishes to refine this talent knows unconditionally that communications need to be verified. Such spiritual discernment is necessary for the channel as well as for those who work with and use the information that is channeled.

There are many ways in which a communication can be verified. One is by having others in or outside of that group receive a similar message or idea. Another is to send the communication to a channel who is respected and who has gone ahead in the techniques and development of this art. Constructive help can be given objectively, and should be taken that way and with love.

Many receive from the same masters or entities on other planes and planets. Therefore, those who operate on that same frequency level can confirm the information by recognizing certain vibratory rates within the message or by recognizing certain thoughts, teachings or hidden keys within the communication.

We urge all to use the chapter on "Spiritual Discernment" in this connection (see page 67). This gives many practical steps for everyone to utilize in determining whether a communication is valid or not, or to discern from what level it has been sent.

Truth has nothing to fear. No harm can occur if one seeks for verification of communications. The masters on the highest planes insist on verification and confirmation. Only those on the lower astral planes criticize or chide those who seek this.

The most perfect measuring rod ever given concerning spiritual activities is the divine law *"By their fruits you will know them."* In other words, if the information does not bear good fruit which nourishes the spiritual development of those involved, then recognize it and grade it accordingly. This is your obligation to your Self and to others.

56

COSMIC MUSIC

When all things began, the Word already was. The Word dwelt with God, and what God was, the Word was. The Word, then, was with God at the beginning, and through Him all things came to be; no single thing was created without Him. — John 1:1–3

The holy scriptures of the Vedas also teach that "the whole cosmic order was brought into manifestation through sound alone."

Man—who is God's creation, the Child made in His image and likeness (essence and qualities)—then was created through the manipulation (movement and rhythm) of sound (words and music). The word *person* in Latin is *personare*, "to sound through."

In her magnificent text *Music: Keynote of Human Evolution*, the New Age teacher, savant and channel Corinne Heline writes: "All life is a vibration. Differentiation is due to the one divine Life vibrating at varying rates. Hence vibration is the key to the secret of both health and sickness, youth and old age, death and its ultimate surrender to immortality.

"The fundamental condition underlying man's well-being is harmony. In obedience to the law of harmony, man was made *in the image and likeness of God.* Trends of the New Day point to man's acceptance of this universal truth, along with an inner realization that it is within his own divine heritage and power to re-create, here and now, conditions in accordance with this initiation pattern."

We know that sound transmutes matter. Even our most materialistic scientists are cognizant of the wonders of sound. A certain sustained pitch or note can break a glass.

Researchers are discovering that music can aid or hinder food-producing animals. Dr. James H. Barrett, the then chairman of Southern Colorado State College's behavioral sciences division, said, "We know that cows give more milk, hens lay more eggs and people buy more in stores when music is played."

Plants respond favorably to classical music, but cringe when exposed to acid rock music, according to researchers at Temple Buell College in Denver, Colorado.

Medical scientists note that music affects the blood flow in the brain independently of the rest of the body. They have recorded that music can produce marked effects on the pulse and the blood pressure, increasing or decreasing muscular energy. Thus they can induce or delay fatigue.

Physicians attending the Second Musical-Therapy Congress in West Berlin during the summer of 1973 claimed that certain types of musical rhythms have been found to be very effective in combating some physical ailments. They have treated stomach ulcers, paralysis and insomnia with music, from the classics to jazz.

But these are facts spiritual scientists long have known. Masters of the art of music have functioned from this premise since the beginning of our known time records.

HISTORY OF MUSIC

Aristotle wrote: "Emotions of any kind are produced by melody and rhythm. Therefore by music, a man becomes accustomed to feeling the right emotion. Music, thus, has power to form character, and the various kinds of music based upon the various modes may be distinguished by their effects on character. One, for example, working in the direction of melancholy, another of effeminacy, one encouraging abandonment, another self-control, enthusiasm, and so on through the series."

Phythagoras—who, according to my channelings, was an incarnation of Serapis Bey, Director of the Fourth Ray of Crystallization-Decrystallization—was among the first to use musical therapy to cure every type of illness of body, mind and soul.

Plato—who, according to my channelings, was Paul the Apostle, and in the etheric Hierarchy of this solar system is Hilarion, Director of the Fifth Ray of Healing, Balance and Unity—insisted: "The plan we have been laying down for youth was well known in Egypt. Namely, nothing but beautiful forms and fine music should be permitted in the assemblies of young people."

In early India, music was used for healing. According to some legends, adepts there were able to tame wild animals and to affect the elements, such as bringing rain for their crops.

India, which has developed forty disciplines of yoga (union with the God Self), has the path of Nada Yoga, the yoga of sound. This brings one an attunement with elemental cosmic energy, through the use of repeated sounds, chants, mantras or songs.

In Greece, music was played by the initiate priesthood. Music and poetry were correlated for mystic purposes, with each poetic line being accompanied by its proper musical note. According to Corinne Heline, "hundreds of musicians every day sang Apollo's [Sonship aspect of God] praises and demonstrated the power of music to affect weather conditions, the growing of plants and the flowing of streams."

Philo, in recording the nocturnal vigils of the early Christians, wrote: "After supper their sacred songs began. When all were risen they selected from the rest two choirs, one of men and one of women, and from each a person of majestic form and well skilled in music to lead the band. They chanted hymns in honor of God, composed in different measures and modulations, now singing together and then answering each other by terms."

Primitive peoples on the American continents and throughout Africa, as well as primitive island tribes such as in Bali and Hawaii, demonstrate profound occult learning in the application of music to nature. They used, and still use, in many areas rain chants and special songs handed down for generations to help increase the productivity of their crops.

MUSIC IN THE AQUARIAN AGE

From my channelings, we have the following mental telepathic communications regarding the use of music and sound in the Aquarian Age, as dictated by two of the directors (chohans) of the Hierarchal Board.

El Morya is Director of the First Ray of Will, Power, Word of God. Serapis Bey is the Director of the Fourth Ray of Crystallization and Decrystallization, under whose direction the art of music is developed. A ray is a spiritual step or aspect in the seven steps of cosmic creation. (See Mark-Age booklet *Seven Rays of Life* and book *MAPP* to Aquarius: *Mark Age Period & Program.*)

&

"The power and the consciousness are one and the same. The consciousness of God is power, energy, force and will. It becomes the spoken word.

"Why must I apply the word *spoken* to the idea or word of God? *Spoken* in this case merely means it is expressed or in action. The word, itself–which is the idea of God for a form or a change or an expression–is not in motion until it has been spoken. By that, it has to be outlined. Whether it is outlined in the mind by the individual or whether it is outlined in a written or verbalized message is really of no consequence.

"Naturally, the spoken-aloud message or decree has the most power or has the most energy behind it, because there is indeed the most force in the sound application. Within sound we have light vibration that is carried within it; an impetus. That light then comes into form by the fact that we apply the verbal or vocalized force or form of the idea that is mentioned.

"It is for this reason, naturally, that we encourage and project through our channels spoken messages and the songs and the music that are much needed during these Latter Days, or the Mark Age period and program. Many, many decrees are pronounced through the sound vibration, even when the words themselves are not consciously understood by the channel or the individual who speaks them.

"The same applies to music. In the Golden Age much music must be used for this particular purpose so the new forms can carry with them this added energy secretion from the Godhead and from the consciousness and from the form of mankind who produces the sound, whether it be in the form of an instrument or through the vocal box of the individual via word, via messages, via song.

"So, we are well pleased when individuals exercise this within themselves. Not only does the sound project and produce a change within the frequency of the person's body who makes it or who hears it, but this sound goes forth and actually creates a certain degree of change within the cellular structure of all animated life upon the planet; depending on the strength of the mind power, the consciousness of the individuals, who use the sound in music or vocalizing the expression.

"So, consciousness is the greatest step and the most important. Depending on the consciousness of the individual, we can broadcast the sound to a larger degree or to a greater segment of the structures or forms that must be influenced. By doing this we have created an endless chain of reactions. By doing this we have secreted power, the idea of God, into the

EL MORYA
Materialization of divine power
Drawing courtesy of Owen Morrison

present form that must be dissolved and re-created into a new form or higher dimension.

"That is what we are referring to in this entire discourse. We are desirous of creating a new form and a new body for each individual and for all life form—animal, vegetable and mineral form—within the planetary structure. As this is done we simultaneously effect those subtle changes within the auric field of the planet and those souls which surround the planet, as given to you in prior discourses, resulting in an appreciation of those astral forms and forces that must be raised along with all Earth planetary creatures and structures."

– El Morya; January 15, 1968

"It is possible to fulfill and to master the four initial steps of the four rays [spiritual aspects] in yourself while on the physical dimension. The three that follow may occur after a third dimensional

61

experience and make you master of the third dimension even though you have not mastered the seven steps [or rays] in a physical environment or body. . . .

"The fourth step, which represents the fulfillment of a physical man, is in the intellectual or mind matter. . . . It is then the doorway of physical into spiritual. That is why it comes through the mental realm or the mind sphere. . . . Let me say that because this fourth step represents the supreme in mental conquering, it is a most difficult one for most of your scientific, philosophic and musical applications, since it represents an intuitive quality as well. It must be a balance with physical and metaphysical. It is always representing that in-between state. It represents that which ponders the physical and goes beyond the physical.

"That is why those who fall under this influence or are in the process of conquering or demonstrating this particular aspect are torn between the two worlds and often are unbalanced in their own concept. But the concept of the fourth step, which is the Fourth Ray of understanding and demonstrating truth as it is in the overall divine plan, is to be the crystal through which man can enter either the physical or the metaphysical world. I use here the term *metaphysical* to mean that which does not rely on a third dimensional vibration. . . .

"The musical sciences are yet to be explored, because they have a frequency range that can be applied to every single apparatus in your environment. Every single attitude of fulfillment, every single crystallized form on the third dimension has its counterpart in a tone or a frequency note. . . .

"The New Age, or the Mark Age period which precludes the Golden Era, mostly will be working with sound vibrations in order to effect those necessary appliances that will aid and will bring about a higher demonstration of the third and the fourth dimensions. I ask then that those who are inclined to bring forth the new appliances, the new equipment for your New Age works, concentrate on the sound aspect of that which is in the ethers for you to bring forth."

— *Serapis Bey; February 27, 1963*

"The same cells within an organ of your body, relating to the same cells in the same organ of another person's body, are in a sense related and unique and individual and regularly, conceptionally figured to be of a same type, interchangeable in some cases from one body to another. But yet, examining them minutely according to our standards, the cellular structure, the atomic difference remain unique in those comparable cells, so that at times they can be in harmony with another and at other times they will not be in harmony with another, even though they will be transplanted or transferred. . . .

"Each atom of life has its own unique sound. When we collect the mineral deposits upon the planet and form begins to manifest into unique cellular structures or crystallized products—you would call them gems, mineral deposits, for other purposes and so forth—an idea, a thought or a desire is implanted with the sound vibration. For this is what the sound carries. It is the word, unique unto that particular crystal or mineral form. Therefore, each mineral and each form of each mineral has its own unique personal concept or energy thought-pattern, and is emitted via this subtle sound, which is the word for it.

"You on the Earth can utilize this information and this concept with music, sound, thought-into-sound or vocalization, which means your conversations, and also into your works via gems and creative products that can carry the frequency of sound. This does include the hieronics [hierarchal vibratory radiations through electromagnetic equipment] concept and schematic, that must include gemlike qualities which will have the property of individualized thought forms instilled in them.

"As you are carried along into this new production you will be taught via the inner planes and by your own Christ intunement. You will be shown step by step how to instill thought form, the proper thought form, the constructive and creative thought form, into those gems or crystals which can emit constantly the desired effect upon you, upon all form and life in the planetary sphere. This is what the Fourth Ray function is to contribute and to hold steadfast while transmutation of life takes place upon Earth planet."

— Serapis Bey; February 26, 1969

DEMONSTRATIONS OF CHANNELING COSMIC MUSIC

Channels such as myself and others of the Mark-Age organization have been demonstrating the ancient art and science of channeling the sounds and the rhythms of cosmic music directly from
our own I Am consciousness and from the masters on the etheric
(Christ) and celestial (angelic) realms.

The things that I do, you shall do, and even greater things. This was the
promise of the great Master, way shower and pattern maker for
Christ consciousness of Earth, Jesus of Nazareth; who, on the etheric planes and in the solar system government, is known by his
cosmic name, Sananda.

Now, during this Mark Age—which is the Latter Days, or the end
of this pattern of material, mortal expression—the spiritual demonstrations of the Christ
Self in action are being
developed to help man
back to his natural heri-
tage and powers as the
Son of God.

MARK & YOLANDA, 1962
When my cosmic singing began,
Mark acted as the battery for the force field

Even though in this
incarnation I cannot read
music or play an instru-
ment, since July 4, 1962,
when I rise into the I Am
state of consciousness I
execute vocal techniques
which even profession-
ally trained singers would
hesitate to perform in
public. The range coming through me is considered by experts to
be extraordinary.*

Some who have heard these cosmic songs have had awakenings
within their own consciousness. Some seem to recall the words or

---

* A selection of my channeled cosmic singing, *My Soul Sings,* is available on
audiocassette through Mark-Age (C-90 tape for $5).

the music, as though they had sung them somewhere else, in some past experience or incarnation; or they seem able to tune in to the same etheric wavelength as I do, and they themselves channel the cosmic songs with me. Others have reported instantaneous healings.

In early 1963 I predicted: "Great choruses and orchestras are being prepared to amplify this power and strength contained in the decrees and invocations that my I Am Self is singing through me. Others, who come in contact with this spiritual talent, will begin to bring forth cosmic music."

This prophecy has been fulfilled many times since then by other Mark-Age channels.

Other Mark-Age channels and I also demonstrate the universal sign language. This is the movement of the hands and the arms, predominantly but also all other parts of the body, in responding to the silent sounds of Spirit which manifest in rhythm and movement.

Every cell of the body radiates energy or vibration. Therefore, each part of the body is transmitting a particular kind of energy or sound or rhythm.

Through this universal sign language, silent messages are transmitted to the cosmic mind, the superconscious, of those present; and, in fact, to the subconscious of all mankind on the planet. Mark-Age channels thus often record for the Hierarchy silent decrees and invocations to bring about the upliftment and the awakening of the I Am Self of others on Earth.

The transmitting of spiritual sound and movement is an ancient art, from the beginning of time, practiced in the lost civilizations of Earth and on other spheres and dimensions of this solar system and beyond. Once again it is being reawakened in this Mark Age period and program for the preparation of man in the coming Aquarian Age, so he can live and can demonstrate as the child of God which he is, always has been and always shall be.

SPIRITUAL DISCERNMENT

We are in a New Age of physical, mental and spiritual unfold-ment on Earth. One of the signs of this time or marks of this age is the great influx of interdimensional and interplanetary communica-tions through highly trained channels. Just because it is an excep-tional rather than a general gift, no one has the right to discard or to ignore this God-given talent and function of the I Am Self. But spiri-tual standards and measuring rods are *necessary* to aid I Am Nation citizens in properly discerning what is true from what is partly true or completely false.

COMMUNICATIONS

Communications are necessary in the present stage of evolution on the Earth because man is not operating in his proper Sonship role, which is Christ in action. Those on the etheric (ascended spheres) project messages of the truth. Those on the astral planes (spheres immediately beyond the physical, five-sensual, three-dimensional frequency) also project to the Earth. And those incar-nated on Earth, masters and others, also transmit. There are light workers in all realms. But how do we know from what level of con-sciousness or evolvement a communicant is speaking, regardless of the plane from which he or she projects?

1. Love is the key and must be the theme! Positive or Father principle of divine love gives strength, justice, cleansing, righteous action and thinking; negative or Mother principle shows wisdom, understanding, compassion, forgiveness, healing and faith. Those in the ascended and celestial realms are perfectly balanced in male and female aspects and can project either or both, depending on the need.

2. The material must be based on divine laws, on light/

love/life-giving principles in constructive action. Love, truth, justice, equal opportunity, freedom, unity and brotherhood are of the essence of Spirit. When man transposes them into this physical plane he often creates limited, restricted laws to control his fellow-men.

3. The material must not contradict truth. Truth is not theory, dogma or interpretation; such are attempts at analyzing truth and are strictly intellectual, often emotional. It may be an authentic contact, but just because a soul continues on to another dimension does not mean it becomes perfected or elevated in consciousness. If the message contradicts factual information that has come through that channel previously, or what is known to you from other channels, be sure to reexamine both objectively.

4. The message must satisfy the inner, give you a desire to grow and to expand your own consciousness. If it conflicts with your own ideas and feelings, question whether your preconceived notions are based on immutable spiritual truth, on intellectual analysis or on the results of preconditioning from family, friends, or background situations of race, nation, religion, and so forth. It is not wrong for a message to disturb you, but on what level are you disturbed? The spiritual you can never shake from its foundation—but the intellectual, physical, mortal self can and must be transmuted. This is a basic purpose of communicating.

5. The information must complement and supplement material coming from others. No one is the only true channel for any work or service of a cosmic nature. Verifications, complementing and supplementing ideas, and instructions are available through many others. But not all of them necessarily work in this particular manner of channeling communications. There are dedicated Christ light instruments working in government, education, medicine, science, industry, the public media of communications and entertainment, and so on.

MASTERS

Be logical, be sensible, do not give up your intellectual reasoning powers before you feel secure and firm on the spiritual foundation.

Learn the meanings of: *cosmic, ascended, spiritual, mastership*. Does the communication you are reviewing live up to those definitions?

1. A master of the etheric planes is above and beyond common, everyday, Earthly type desires, reasonings, explanations and concerns. If you can procure the information contained in the message through the usual Earth plane sources, then obviously there is no need for an ascended master to speak through channeled communications.

2. Masters do not resort to vicious attacks or character defamation. They do point out error, but they know that all are subject to it, past or present, and therefore constructive rather than destructive criticism is always the only method used. Anyone using destructive criticism is not operating at that moment in a Christ, but rather in an anti-Christ, manner. The Christ way is to stress and to work to bring forth the light, not to concentrate on darkness. This is a trap many light workers fall into.

GLO-RIA

Ascended masters, such as depicted in this painting by Vera Leeper, use constructive, never destructive, teaching methods

3. What mortal consciousness considers a problem or an obstacle is considered by ascended consciousness as a challenge or an opportunity for soul experience, growth and service.

4. Cosmic masters come to all in the cosmos. They are available, one way or another, to all who sincerely seek them. They do not work solely with one group, one race, one nation or one ideology. They may concentrate their activities but they are never exclusive with one individual or group.

5. Ascended masters do not give specific solutions to the usual mortal or Earth plane problems. They may suggest solutions but they never do the work for you. Those on Earth have come to do the physical work; those on the higher realms guard, guide, aid, and have their own work to do. The various planes cooperate and coordinate, but they cannot perform the functions of the others, for all planes have been created by Spirit for their own purposes.

6. Master teachers are mainly concerned with spiritual instruction. They do not interfere with your freewill choices. They offer or lead you to opportunities for expression or expansion and they allow you the freedom to make mistakes or to benefit from your own achievements. If you ask ascended masters to make judgments or decisions for you, they will give you spiritual laws by which you must reach your own conclusions. They state spiritual facts. You are then free to apply them according to your own understanding and conscience. By the divine law of cause and effect they cannot tell anyone what to do or to think. So beware of alleged masters who deliver detailed instructions telling you what to do, where to go, and how to put into action the role of your own God Self.

7. Those in Christ consciousness work for one thing: to bring all others into that consciousness and demonstration. Ascended masters are not interested in glory for their own achievements or accomplishments, but they do wish to help all to achieve eternally increasing expression of the glory of God. They do not attempt to bind or to limit their disciples, but do seek to help them learn the truth and gain the experience that sets them free to manifest as children of God in their own right.

Remember that one in mortal consciousness is not able to understand fully or to instruct ascended masters. Unfortunately, many truth students err here.

CHANNELS

Channel is the current term for psychic, sensitive, oracle, seer, medium, prophet. The highest form of channeling communications from another dimension (which is simply thought transference or mental telepathy) is in the fully conscious awareness. However, those who go into deep trance or semi-suspended states can be of equally valuable service; it is a matter of experience and purpose. It takes many lives, on the Earth plane and other dimensions, to enable one to become proficient and dependable in demonstrating this spiritual talent.

Some channels also demonstrate healing, levitation, materialization and dematerialization, bilocation and other gifts. Not all have earned all gifts and some specialize only in one. The most any channel can hope for is to become a crystal-clear, open vessel for the Christ Self within, an instrument through whom communicants on other frequencies can project themselves in thought, in energy or in actual physical demonstrations. This is the dual responsibility of a communications channel, who must be a living example of what is taught.

Here are some of the *pitfalls, errors* and *false illusions* which endanger every channel, be he or she a channel just for his/her own high Self or for other communicants also:

1. The Earth atmosphere is dense and distorted. Fourth dimensional senses have difficulty in relating and adjusting to this three-dimensional, five-sensual, material world.

2. Channels are influenced by the mental projections of others. This includes group thought-forms, be they occult patterns and paths, religious beliefs, or national and racial heritages. All thoughts become part of the subconscious track. Unless they are reexamined and reevaluated continually, they may color the discourses and messages.

3. The ego personality of the individual self is an accumulation of karmic patterns from this and past lives. Personality interferences are obvious in messages expressing indignation, anger, retribution, hurt, pity, sympathy, threats, isolated independence, complaints, sarcasm, downgrading, bragging, excuses or justifications, and other such non-Christ actions.

Each of the preceding categories has to be examined and cleansed by those who sincerely work for their own Self-realization, as well as by those who work toward clear channeling of interdimensional and interplanetary forces. Those who attack or seek to destroy the channel or the work of the channel, or who ridicule the

MARK & YOLANDA, 1968
*Spiritual discernment always has been a
key theme of our metaphysical teachings*

technique of channeling itself, only reveal their own ignorance, insecurity and fear of what they do not understand or cannot properly demonstrate. Even for those who are spiritually open and aware, there are higher levels of evolvement and action which they may not accept or fully comprehend.

Those who resort to viciousness and defamation of individuals and groups fool and hurt themselves more than others. When you witness this, know that the person is actually blind to Spirit and to Spirit's ways of working. There is undoubtedly a beam in his own eye; he is blaming another for something that is wrong in himself.

The major part of the channeling on the Earth plane now is distorted. How is it possible that a channel who is willing, dedicated and trained for many lifetimes can deliver false communications and distorted views or can be clear some of the time and out of focus at other times?

One can only blame one's self for being deceived if one does not use the God-given sense of inner verification and spiritual discrimination. One cannot be expected to know all at once, but one must be perceptive and willing to learn. Though the answers to this question are varied, complicated and far from complete at this time, here are a few of the considerations to meditate upon. Keep in mind that a channel is a living instrument for communication, such as the telephone, radio or television. If an inanimate mechanical object can develop flaws and be subject to interference, static or debris, imagine how much more so can the human channel with its multiple levels, parts and functionings.

1. *Subconscious* of the channel can interfere, put up blocks or play tricks. Knowing the background, education, environment, past-life experiences, associates, motives and degree of demonstration of the I Am Self is often necessary before final judgments of authenticity or grading are possible. Spiritual judgment is not wrong. If you use mortal measurements you will be judged by the standards set by men, but if you gauge with spiritual discernment you will be judged by Christ standards and will reap spiritual fruits according to the law of cause and effect.

2. *Interpretation* by the channel is one of the most subtle and almost imperceptible disturbances. When a communicant is expressing an idea, the channel, whether conscious or in trance, can insert his/her own ideas, feelings or ways of expression on that subject. The message you hear then is not that of the one delivering the talk, but is colored partly or completely by the channel. Codes, unknown or ancient tongues, key words, phrases or prefixes and obsolete meanings are used to keep the channel's conscious thoughts and subconscious memories off the track. It takes great discipline and faith for the channel to bring forth unfamiliar terms.

3. The time element can lead to distortion by the channel. Not all messages are picked up and delivered in the same time segment they are originally transmitted. Channels can tune in to a frequency vibration, pick up prerecorded material and retransmit it. That means the sender is not in personal contact, even though his vibration or presence may be felt. Much error can creep in when the channel is not under the tight control that occurs during original transmission.

4. A channel who is mentally, emotionally or physically upset should *never* attempt contact. The hazards under those circumstances are tremendous. It is not worth the risk, unless there is an emergency. Ascended masters never channel through a disturbed instrument, for they know only distortion would result.

5. Once a channel has slipped off the track and his physical-mental-emotional equipment goes out of focus, he has to be realigned. Many do not know they have been thrown out of alignment, and continue to work in distortion, even for years. Many continue to deliver messages allegedly from the masters which are not in reality from such. Masters do not interfere with the freewill choice of channels and those associated with them because they know certain soul lessons are being achieved, even if not realized until another lifetime. A master never creates an error situation, fools a channel or delivers wrong information deliberately in the form of a test. Such is the antithesis of the ascended state of consciousness. These claims are but self-justifications for error channeling.

6. The level of contact varies according to the soul evolvement of the channel and the mission. One who lives an ascended life on the physical plane is capable of channeling the ascended masters from the etheric. If he does not live, teach and demonstrate divine law, then intermediaries or representatives are sent in to make the contact. This fact is usually concealed from the channel. Unfortunately it can result in further phasing down from the direct, clear line of communication, with greater possibility of distortion or misinterpretation from either the physical or intermediary levels.

7. There are more levels of and problems in mental communication than any on Earth at this time can understand. This means there are so many originating or duplicating sources of communication that none here can discern all. One of the greatest dangers is in improperly guided and guarded attempts at mental telepathy between those now on Earth. It is possible and necessary, but only when understood.

Remember, this chapter is not meant to be complete in itself; it is merely a basic guide. A prime purpose of the Mark Age period is to teach and to demonstrate that you are, and must act as, a child of God, Christ in action. Extremely important in this Christ unfoldment are *spiritual discernment* and *discrimination.*

The time of *now* is a divine opportunity to improve these talents that all must utilize in eternal soul evolvement and work. Honestly and sincerely seek attunement with your I Am Self and you will be given the truth.

THE CHURCH
& THE NEW AGE

by Reverend Francis Cuzon
Roman Catholic Priest

If the channelings revealed through Mark-Age are not true, then what the Catholic Church teaches is not true either. . . . What is happening now in the world is that which is being revealed through many channels or prophets in the world, but particularly through Mark-Age.

THE AWAKENING

When did I start in New Age work? I don't know, exactly. I feel there never has been any break with the old. It is the old overlapping into the new. This is the remarkable way God usually makes us grow. The new has to come from the old. The new has to be prepared by the old, while the old gives its essence to the new.

In December 1958 I was coming back from the Far East in order to get more involved in this work for the dawning Aquarian Age, coming from Singapore to Colombo, Ceylon. We arrived in the early morning. When I woke up, I got up and went up on deck, to find out that we already had arrived. But many did not know it, and were still sleeping. I thought: Here we are, after a long trip. These people are going to wake up from their dreams and start anew. Certainly some are going to start new phases of their lives.

Also the thought came to me that this was like the long trip we all had taken together over the centuries: Jews, Catholics, Protestants, Moslems, Hindus, Buddhists. Now we have come to a new phase, a new place in the history of mankind, in the history of God's work on Earth. Very few are aware of it, or even awake yet.

Then I thought: What is going to happen? The Catholics will go to their parish priest and ask him: What are we going to do? He will advise them to be patient, he will have to wait for directives from the bishop. Of course, the bishop will say: Let's wait and see what the Pope says about it. Probably the Pope then will call for a council, which he does on rare, important occasions.

The Protestants will say: We'll turn to the Bible. There they will find a lot of information about what is to come.

The spiritualists have the better part. They have a direct communication system and probably are receiving news from the other side from their beloved ones, saying: All is well; you are coming to a new consciousness, and we are preparing everything for you.

Surely the Jews will say: Our way throughout the centuries has been by following Abraham, Jacob and Isaac. They too will be guided in the right way.

THE ANNOUNCEMENTS

Two months later I was in Rome. I had contacted the Movement for a Better World, which had been started by Pope Pius XII, who was very eager to inaugurate a new-thought movement in the Church. The movement was started by a Jesuit priest who felt that the two worlds, the spiritual and the physical, were blending, that something new was coming.

I was in Rome at St. Paul's on Sunday, the 25th of January, when Pope John XXIII announced the Council. I was also present on Wednesday a few days later when he gave a general audience to the public, saying, "It has been a long time, two thousand years. We are going to start anew." Pope John also had the idea of renewing everything, in order to make the Church an instrument in the hands of Christ to renew everything on the face of the Earth.

Meanwhile, the Jews have accomplished great things, too. They have returned to Jerusalem, coming back home after two thousand years. Now the state of Israel is on the map and very much a part of the great nations of the world. This is one of the signs of the times or marks of this age, and we have to know it.

The Protestants recently have been looking more deeply into the Bible and have had a reawakening. The spiritualist movement continues giving good news from the other world. Out of this belief,

New Age groups have sprung up. In higher aspects, we now have expert channels in interdimensional communications.

Personally, I have met a lot of New Age groups and have read a lot of material, but nowhere do I find anywhere in the world better material or better channels than we have in Mark-Age. I am very honored and privileged to be able to work with all of the Mark-Age staff and Family throughout the world who help and who prepare this great work, to disseminate it to the world.

In Japan you find millions of people coming into the New Age. There are New Age churches with millions of members. There is one group that started in the nineteenth century, which also received the information that this Aquarian Age is to come. So, you see throughout the world today many things have been happening, even in our lifetime.

ROMAN CATHOLIC CHURCH

Pope Paul VI was much aware of the things that were coming, and sometimes was disturbed by the way people reacted. Some Catholics think that because we have changed the dress of the priests and nuns we have entered into the New Age. There is much more than that to this. Anyone can learn all about it through the Mark-Age literature and the University of Life.

A message of hope came from Pope Paul on Easter Sunday, 1971: "Not only is the cause of man not lost but it is in a good position. The great ideas which have been the light of the world throughout the centuries will ever shine. The world will find its way to unity. A new human order, a new civilization, is coming. A new age is dawning upon us."

The Pope prepares in advance everything he utters publicly. So, when he speaks of a "new human order" he certainly gave deep thought to the subject. In the spring of 1972 he recommended that the new bishops be chosen from among men who are attentive to the signs of the times, because he knows these are very important times and we have to watch what is happening and watch what Spirit is doing.

The first time I officially heard of the New Age was in 1937. I was only seventeen years old. Those were quite hard times for those who believed in the spiritual world. Pius XI had managed to have his encyclical read in every church in Germany on the same day during the same ten o'clock mass, condemning Nazism.

Meanwhile, at the same time the Pope was speaking to a Congress of Youth in Rome: "Happy are you, the young people, because you shall see great things. We are living during the birth of a new world, and you young people will see all these things coming in your lifetime." I must say this was a great encouragement to us, because some of us feared the light of Spirit would be delayed another three hundred or four hundred years more, expecting probably that Communism would envelop Europe and bring us through another dark age again.

Pius XI also was quite clear in his statement two weeks before he made his transition. Speaking from Rome to a Congress of Pilgrims at Lourdes over the Vatican radio, he said, "Now, not only do I believe but I *know* that God is going to establish His kingdom on Earth." This is a very strong statement.

When Pope John XXIII came to office, he found the Secret of Fatima, which was supposed to be opened in 1960. Why it was not opened before, he did not know. But obviously he realized we were facing great times, and he too could see the signs or marks of this age, the Mark Age.*

In his encyclical "Peace on Earth," he also asked us to look for the signs of the times. Then he called for a council to reform the Catholic Church so it might become a mark of reconciliation among men and that we all may become again the children of one God upon this Earth. From these higher authorities in the Church I find encouragement and verifications that the Catholic hierarchy is preparing the Church for the Age of Aquarius.

HISTORY OF MASS EDUCATIONAL PROGRAM

The Catholic Church transformed the Roman Empire; a great work, when you consider transforming people's hearts, or at least changing something of their outer attitudes. This was after three hundred years of persecution when so many souls already had given

---

* See the following chapter, "Mary Heralds Second Coming."

their lives for Christ and had gone on the other side to help. This started the first mass educational program. As everyone knows, educating the mass population of all Earth is no easy or simple task.

The fathers of the Church in the fourth century—and the Church dogma has been based from what they said, what they talked about: the sermons of St. Augustine, St. Ambrose, St. Basil, St. Gregory—started the first really great mass educational program on Earth. We pray for them to help us again in this age.

The Church at that time had just started its program, when the invasions by the barbarians halted all progress. The Roman Empire fell, and the barbarians from the East were transformed or converted from this interchange of peoples and ideas. The history of many nations in Europe—Germany, France, Austria, Hungary, Romania—started from these times. All of these masses of people were changed. They would not be what they are now if the Church had not done its great educational work then.

Of course, the Church knew then that the outside work was important also, just as spiritual leaders know now. But the most important part is what was done then and is being done now in the hearts of people, in the silence of each one's soul. That is how the monastic orders started, and they have been going on for centuries.

The Benedictines, for instance, working and praying, are not talked about very often, but throughout the centuries they have been the light of the world for many souls. Also, they had been waiting for centuries for the dawn of this New Day, for the manifestation of the sons of God on Earth, knowing that one day God would materialize all His promises to His children.

In the thirteenth century marvelous cathedrals were built throughout Europe as centers of prayer and study. They are living witnesses to that great time of spreading the truths to the entire known world.

By the sixteenth century came the Reformation. At first they tried to make things better, but the Church divided. Some became Protestants, some went on being Catholics. But never has it been the same again.

Deep in our hearts we feel that this division must now be ended. We know this is the will of God, because we know that Jesus himself prayed that all of us be as one, just as the Father and he are one.

THE NEW JERUSALEM

A short time later a new adventure began. People started coming to a new world. Christopher Columbus, bearer of the Christ light, left Spain and came to America. This also was a move by the Spirit of God to start anew, to break from the old, to make a new link with heaven. During the first fourteen centuries many souls died for the Christ light. But dying physically is not necessarily a bad thing, because it forces the soul to start again. Otherwise, most would just stick to the old and not grow. Therefore, God sometimes has to deal harshly with our old ruts and ideas, just to get us out of them and to make us begin anew.

This was the beginning of a great adventure, a new life, a new world, contacting a great civilization that was developed here by the American natives. This certainly was intended to be the beginning of a new world order, the start of the New Jerusalem. Unfortunately, it failed in many respects.

So, we have to start again, just like we always have done throughout the centuries. Now we know this is the right time. This time it will not fail, because of the mass educational program from the higher planes reaching all peoples in the world simultaneously, like the program through Mark-Age and the University of Life. This is a great encouragement.

I do not deny the mistakes made by the Church. When I was at school, one argument given to us to prove that God was with the Church was: The Church has made so many mistakes that if God had not been with us it would have disappeared a long time ago.

Let us therefore not be afraid of admitting our mistakes. The Church, like all else on Earth, is made up of human beings. And human beings are of all kinds and all levels of spiritual understanding and development.

But through all our mistakes the Spirit of God has been able to work great and wonderful things, because behind the scenes always there have been the silent watchers. The silent watchers are the Earth's externalization of the esoteric White Brotherhood (as opposed to the dark forces), part of the spiritual Hierarchy's mass educational program.

Jesus wanted the things of truth to be said to the public. He wanted everybody to know the truth, for the truth is to set humanity free. But even in the time of Jesus there were mystery schools. There were people saying: These truths are not meant for the public, they are not meant for a mass educational program, but just for a few. However, Jesus started that mass educational program by saying: Take this good news to all the four corners of the world. So, throughout the ages there have been the silent watchers on Earth preparing and working in the hearts of people.

This new civilization coming, this new order, the New Jerusalem, is not a religion. It is a way of life. The underground, esoteric White Brotherhood never has tried to start new religions, but rather to bring a way of life that makes us live *within* God; not to pray *to* God, not to kneel down before God, but *to be one with Him,* letting Him be one within us in teaching us how to enter into the house of God. The house of God is our bodies, minds and souls.

This great Brotherhood was in action at the time of Jesus, and prepared the way for Jesus. You have heard of the Dead Sea scrolls. There is much more to be published on these than already has been published to date. These hidden truths will be revealed in these Latter Days, the Mark Age period and program.

Back in the thirteenth century in Europe, behind the scenes, the White Brotherhood inspired the Order of the Temple, the Knight Templars. They claim to have been in action in the times of David and Solomon, as well as at the time of Jesus. Their work was to build the temple of God in each one of us. They are the ones who built those marvelous cathedrals which helped to instruct the whole continent of Europe in understanding that God's presence is everywhere seen.

Now, after six hundred years of silence, the Order of the Temple is again in action in Europe. In the Middle Ages they had nine thousand centers! You can imagine what nine thousand centers today will do when they come into action during this present time.

TODAY'S WORK

Now what is really happening? We are entering the Age of Aquarius. There are the twelve signs of the Zodiac. Our solar sys-

81

tem moves from one sign to the other every 2,160 years. Just twenty-six thousand years ago we also had passed through the Age of Aquarius, and now we return to it again.

Aquarius is the sign of water. *Aqua* in Latin means "water." When water is poured on our Earth, everything we have sown comes to life. Therefore, all the things of the past are springing up to the surface. Everything that is deep in the heart of each one of us is being revealed. We have to discriminate between what we want to keep and what we want to reject. These are our judgments to make.

To the Jews it is quite clear that we are coming to the messianic age. According to certain calculations, the great sabbatic period started in October 1944. Strangely enough, those were the times when the concentration camps opened. That certainly was a time of great darkness for a great sabbath.

The word *sabbath* means the Spirit of God entering into all structures to change them, to transmute them, even to make them entirely new. That is why the Jews have every Saturday as the Sabbath, because they want to start the new week with the Spirit of God coming into action, changing in them what needs to be changed.

To those who are aware, Aquarius concerns the Second Coming of Christ: the coming of the Christ consciousness into all of us, into mankind as a whole race. That definitely means the end of the old world. We have built, through our ignorance, through our own human views, a world without God. This, then, is the end of that world. That is definite.

So, those people who see things happening as the end of the world are correct. To others, however, it is just like spring. Everything is born anew. Everything comes to light. Everything is being renewed. The flowers of our spiritual cells are growing again. The trees of our life forms are green again. The life of God in all of us is coming into action.

All the powers that were present in us from the beginning are coming now to wake us up, because *now is the time*. Two thousand years ago it was too early. Just like my ship docking in the court of Colombo harbor at five o'clock in the morning; nobody went around to wake up the people, because they knew we'd have to wait until nine o'clock to land. Now, this Mark Age period, is the time to wake up everyone. And, of course, many people are waking up.

These signs of things to come are not occurring suddenly. We have been given a grace period, which has been called the Mark Age. It is the age of the signs or marks of this age, to prepare ourselves. Just like on that ship before landing, we have to prepare ourselves. On waking up, all passengers first will clean up and put on their new clothes. Then they must look for their passports, because they will be asked for their identities, who they are, where they are going. Often this is the most confusing time, because some may have misplaced their passports, and because so many people do not know who they really are. This is rather painful, not to know who you are.

MARK AGE PERIOD

When the people come to remember why they are here on Earth, they will want information about this new world and new life order. That is why the mass educational program, such as through Mark-Age's University of Life, has prepared this information for everybody: where they come from, where they are supposed to go, what they are, what is the New Age, and then what they all must do to cooperate with one another.

So, we all have to be attentive to the signs of the times. We have to examine all the messages being given to us, with an open mind. As far as the Catholics are concerned, there have been many calls throughout the past years. Since the early nineteenth century, there have been numerous manifestations of the Blessed Mother Mary nearly every ten years, and recently more often than that. She is preparing us now, as she did in giving birth to Jesus, that the Christ is within ourselves. She heralds the Christ coming, first in our own individual consciousnesses and then in the Second Coming of Jesus, who is the Prince of Earth.

In my personal opinion, among the best messages being channeled today are those through the textbooks and regular publications of Mark-Age. If you know anything better than these, just inform the Mark-Age directors, and I am sure they will integrate everything they find of pure value into the curriculum of the University of Life.

To conclude, I believe there is a reality, a spiritual reality, the kingdom of God, that is within us, and that it is peace, order and harmony. I believe that we can commune with this inner reality. *Commune* means to be one with, and also means to express peace, order and harmony in our lives.

I believe it is mankind's destiny to become the medium of expression through which the kingdom of God can work His wonders upon the Earth, while at the same time we evolve that medium into the living image of God.

I believe that the inner reality, God, the kingdom of heaven, is the Creative Energy and substance everywhere present in all. Divine love is the power always available within the consciousness of each person.

I believe that each one of us is not only a child of God, a child of the cosmic, but also master of his or her own life. I believe that we all can be limitless love in action, and that we all can become channels of New Age energies, which will break down all barriers that exist between our fellowmen and the other kingdoms of life.

I believe that it is now possible to establish and to maintain a system of cooperation between the worlds which will lead to peace, order, harmony, and the kingdom of God on Earth.

This chapter is an edited version of a ninety-minute lecture given at the Open Forum of the University of Life in Miami, Florida, January 1972.

MEET FRANCIS CUZON

Reverend Francis Cuzon became a Mark-Age Family member in 1966 and has corresponded continuously with us since that time. Not only has he studied the Mark-Age channelings, but there are few people in the world who are as well acquainted with them for exact content and interpretation. Moreover, he has faithfully translated into French our textbook *1000 Keys to the Truth* (*Mille clés de la vérité,* available in softcover for $10).

Born in 1920 in Brittany, France, he was interested at a very early age in becoming a Catholic priest. At the age of twenty he joined a missionary society, and during World War II was sent to the Far

East as a chaplain. From 1945 to December 1946 he served with the French army in North Vietnam.

From there he went into China as a missionary to help establish missions and a high school. He was in China five years prior to the revolution, then during the revolution was arrested and imprisoned for nine months.

REV. FRANCIS CUZON

"During those nine months," he reflects, "I had a great deal of time to think. I thought: This is the time for my spiritual work, time to link up the East and the West. I think the Chinese are very clever and understand many spiritual things, because one day the soldiers led me out and said they were concerned that one as young as I had a great deal of work to do. They said, 'We have decided to expel you. Are you willing to leave China?' I replied, 'That's a very good idea.'"

From there Francis went to central Malaya, where he founded a Chinese Catholic high school. When he left there in 1958 he traveled throughout Europe, particularly England, for about another year in order to become better acquainted with some of the metaphysical light centers and groups that then were developing and about whom he had heard a great deal during his stay in Malaya.

Then, in 1959, he joined the oldest religious order in Europe, the Abbey of Saint Maurice in Switzerland (founded in A.D. 515). There he served in the abbey and the high school for twelve years.

In 1960, through some channels of the Universal Link, St-Annes-on-sea, U.K., Francis was told that he would come to the United States to begin a special spiritual mission in this area of the world. Although it did not seem likely then that it would work out, he knew and often wrote to us that he was coming to link up with the spiritual Hierarchy of our solar system, through our unit.

On November 11, 1971, he did link physically with Mark and me in California. It was there, and later in 1971 in Miami, that more of his work was outlined for him by Sananda/Jesus, the Master whom he has been serving in the Church for many years in this lifetime and, as we learned, in many lifetimes prior to this incarnation.

It was given to Francis through me and through his own intunements that part of his function is to help bring all churches, not just the Roman Catholic Church, into this New Age. He believes implicitly in this life pattern, and knows he has been preparing for this educational mission for many lives. It was revealed that he worked with Brother Francis of Assisi, who founded the Franciscan order.

While Francis Cuzon was in China, he began to feel a soul-memory recall of the twenty-two California missions. There were twenty-two missions in California, not twenty-one as generally spoken of today; the twenty-second being the city of Los Angeles. Also, there were twenty-two missions because there are twenty-two letters in the Hebrew alphabet.

Therefore, from November 1971 until February 1973 Francis worked spiritually and on the inner to link the twenty-two missions of California with the Eastern missions and work done by the Hierarchy, and to reestablish the basic spiritual purpose for those missions as part of the mass educational program.

From 1973 to 1979 he served at the Abbey of Saint Maurice in Switzerland; then, from 1979 to 1993, in Lausanne as Director of the English-Speaking Roman Catholic Mission. He now resides in Caux. Francis is still a member of the Abbey of Saint Maurice, which has been active in that area since its foundation in A.D. 515.

Please address your correspondence to: Rev. Francis Cuzon, 1824 Caux, Switzerland.

MARY HERALDS
SECOND COMING

PREPARE FOR BIRTH OF CHRIST

Since the early nineteenth century the Blessed Mary has been appearing frequently to prepare mankind for the Second Coming, which refers both to the coming of Christ or cosmic consciousness to the entire race on Earth as well as to the Second Coming of the Master or Prince of this planet, he who was born as Jesus of Nazareth through the virgin, spiritually pure Mary.

In a channeling through me on October 3, 1960, Mary revealed: "There have been many manifestations of my work on the Earth plane in the last one hundred and fifty years. During this time it has been my mission and purpose to prepare the way for the Master Jesus, as you know him in his last incarnation; to bring his message for his return to believers and teachers of this particular Mark Age."

Reading the signs of our times or the marks of this Latter-Day age is one of the great challenges and rewards for spiritual light workers, because in them they are able to see the fulfillment of prophecies which have been with us for approximately the last two thousand years. In a mental telepathic communication through me on October 4, 1960, Jesus explained: "When a teacher or a master, such as Mary, appears and gives prophecy—as was given to the children of Fatima—it is part of a divine plan or program . . . working through a board of teachers or masters over a period of thousands of years . . . which leads up to an ultimate goal." The goal, in this case, is twofold: the Second Coming of Jesus as the Christ of Earth and the coming of man's Christ consciousness. This also is referred to in our literature as the incoming fourth dimension for our planet.

In her October 3rd communication, Mary explained her role and mission: "As in the story of the birth of Jesus, I am the teacher, the example from which the seed [the message] comes forth. Therefore, manifestations of my work and teachings have come forth prior to the teachings of the Son of God [your own holy I Am consciousness and those teachings of Christ Jesus]. . . . I have demonstrated fertility and willingness in the minds of men to receive the message of the Second Coming. . . . The Second Coming is literal as well as spiritual, for the individual person as well as for the race."

The great Catholic scholar and writer St. Louis-Marie Grignion de Montfort (1673–1716), author of *True Devotion to the Blessed Virgin Mary,* wrote: "In the Second Coming of Jesus, Mary has to be made known and revealed by the Holy Ghost, in order that, through her, Jesus Christ may be known, loved and served." Her repeated presence in this and the last century marks an era of Marian Apostolates.

Jesus appeared to Berthe Petit at Pontmain, Belgium, at a midnight mass on Christmas 1909, saying: "The hearts of men must be changed. This will be realized only when devotion to the sorrowful and immaculate heart of Mary is known, developed, preached and counseled everywhere. This is the last aid which God gives to the world before the end time [the Latter Days, or Mark Age]."

Mary herself relayed via mental telepathic communication through me on November 7, 1962: "Now is my time for actual demonstration and participation. I am coming forth in many ways. It has been known for many hundreds of years that my part in the scheme of this race's evolution is to be made manifest."

A further explanation came through me on July 5, 1961, by Dr. Hannibal, known in other literature as the ascended master St. Germain: "Mary's role is one of great importance, always in relationship to anything having to do with the personality you know as Jesus. Mary's relationship is equally important in the world, or mass consciousness, when working on Christ- or God-conscious evolvement.

"Mary represents the subconsciousness or the mold in which all things are gestated. Do you follow what I am saying? She is the mother in which the seed does grow. She represents that aspect of the God consciousness, as Jesus represents the male or the active force, bringing it forth. So, she represents the nourishing part of God's seed, always remembering that each one is a representative

88

and a part of the whole, serving each other part of the whole.

"Her role at this time is the same as it was during the life of Jesus. She nurtured the seed for nine months—and many years, of course, after his birth—as the physical mother. But she also is nurturing the seed of mankind by her special work in the etheric for the last two thousand years; and will continue until all men are brought into Christ-conscious awareness." So it is that Mary has been called the World Mother or the Mother of God, meaning the womb or the way through which God consciousness is born in man.

DOCUMENTED APPEARANCES OF MARY

Mary, being an ascended master, expressing universal consciousness and divine love, is no respecter of historical times, individual positions, personal honor or glory, specific religions, races or nationalities. Thus her appearances and messages are given to peasants, priests, working men and women, children, journalists and prophets among Muslims, Christians and Jews.

In the past two centuries her appearances or demonstrations of her intervening powers have been chronicled in detail. The following examples do not include the hundreds of teachings and communions through soul-to-soul contact or mental telepathic communication, which are as legitimate spiritual unions as the more physical ones. As a matter of fact, most spiritual scriptures, such as the Old and New Testaments, are based on inspired writings and dictations which in our modern vernacular we call channelings.

The child Mari Loli of Garabandal, Spain, reports that Mary explained: "I am not here with you in body and soul but in another form." This form is the Blessed Lady's ascended or light body, which all may expect to express in the next evolutionary period on Earth, the Golden Age of Aquarius.

- 1830, Our Lady of Paris, France, appeared to nun Sister Catherine Laboure.

- 1846, La Salette, France, to Mélanie Calvat (14) and to Maximin Giraud (11).

- 1858, Lourdes, France, as seen by Bernadette Soubirous (14).

- 1871, Pontmain, France, alerting four children to apparitions in local church seen by one third of the population.
- 1876, Marpingen near Treves, Germany.
- 1877, Dietrichswalde in Eastern Prussia.
- 1880 in New Pompeii, Italy, where Mary expressed through a miraculous picture.
- 1916–17 in Fatima, Portugal, to Lucia dos Santos (10), Francisco Marto (9), and his sister Jacinta (7).
- 1946 in Marienfried, Germany, visions by Barbara Reuss; witnessed by Reverend Martin Rumpf and his sister Anna.
- 1953 in Syracuse, Sicily, Mary's plaster image wept profusely for days; owned by Antonia Giusto, a sickly, twenty-year-old, newly married, pregnant woman who was cured.
- 1961–65 in Garabandal, Spain, to Mari Loli (12), Conchita (12), Jacinta (12), and Mari Cruz (11).
- 1968–71 in Zeitun, suburb of Cairo, Egypt, frequent apparitions at St. Mary's Church were witnessed by more than a million people of all faiths.
- February 1971 in Maropti, Italy; painting of Our Lady of Pompeii wept human blood, forming crosses on the wall under the picture.
- 1981, and frequently for years following, in Medjugorje (former Yugoslavia), to two boys and four girls, ages ten to seventeen; messages included ten prophecies ("secrets"), containing chastisements, warnings and a miraculous sign; reported apparitions and messages continue to this day.
- 1983 to mid-1980s, in Shoubra, suburb of Cairo, Egypt, frequent apparitions of "a woman clothed in light" at Church of St. Damian were witnessed by thousands, as at Zeitun.

When I was in the I Am consciousness or my Nada state on April 7, 1969, I recorded: "An ascended master can independently appear upon the Earth, just as Mary has appeared many, many times and is appearing right at this moment upon the Earth to many who will open their eyes to see and to accept her warnings, her teachings and her pleadings with mankind to return unto his first step and first initiation, which is the birth of the Son [Christ] consciousness."

The statement "right at this moment upon the Earth" referred to Mary's frequent apparitions near Cairo, Egypt, from the night of April 2–3, 1968, through early 1971. According to ancient legends, these appearances were approximately in the area where she and Joseph had fled with the infant Jesus when Herod was searching for and killing all males of two years and under because the prophets had proclaimed the birth of the Messiah, the true King of Israel.

MARY APPEARS AS LIGHT

Mary's appearances at the Church of St. Mary usually were heralded by mysterious lights. So bright was her illumination that spectators found it impossible to distinguish her features. Some described these lights as fluorescent or sheet lightning, others as a "circle of bright spotlights," "falling stars" or "a shower of diamonds of lights" which swirled in the path of her movements. Sometimes a brilliant crown of lights was seen over her head, giving her a glorious majesty.

All who have seen Mary in this extraordinary, supranatural way emphasize the light around her. Similarly, shepherdess child Mélanie Calvat on September 19, 1846, in La Salette, France, described her vision: "It seemed as if the moving light increased or rather became concentrated all round the most holy Virgin

APPARITION OF MARY
Actual photograph of Mary atop St. Mary's Church, Zeitun, Egypt

to prevent my seeing her anymore. Thus the light took the place of those parts of the body which disappeared from before our eyes; or rather it seemed that the body of my Lady changed into light as it melted away. The ball of light rose gently upwards. I cannot say whether the amount of light diminished as it rose or if it was merely the distance which caused the light to grow fainter as it moved farther away until it disappeared altogether."

Another phenomenon witnessed many times was mainly associated with Mary's appearances in Egypt, that of lights surrounding or heralding her appearances. During and after the Virgin's appearances, and sometimes on nights when she did not come at all, there appeared flights of strange luminous birds which were not part of the Earth world, since they flew too fast and without moving their wings.

On June 1, 1968, she appeared as a light in the center of the opening beneath the small dome. In a tape interview by Jerome Palmer, O.S.B., Bishop Gregorius, nondiocesan bishop for the Higher Studies in the Coptic Culture and Scientific Research, stated: "The light took the shape of a sphere, moving up and down. Then slowly it moved out through the supporting archway and took the form of the holy Virgin. It lasted two or three minutes and as usual the people shouted to her. She usually acknowledges their greetings with both hands, or with one, if she should be holding the olive branch or the Christ child. She seems happy and smiling, always kindly, but somewhat sad."

MARY'S WARNINGS TO MANKIND

Mary's messages have two things in common. First, they are universal and meant as warnings and preparations for all people on the Earth without exception. Secondly, they repeatedly beg for repentance (being truly sorry for one's mistakes and resolving to change one's ways), and they warn that if this does not come there will be cleansing cataclysms, followed later by a great miracle performed by Jesus which all on Earth will know about and will see. Bear in mind that the manner, the language and even the demonstrations always are according to what the individual(s) can comprehend and relate to in environment, training and background.

As Mary channeled through me on October 3, 1960, "For the past one hundred and fifty years I have demonstrated fertility and willingness in the minds of men to receive the message of the Second Coming. This is the prophecy of Fatima."

To the three children in Fatima, Mary announced: "The Lord is offended. Pray for the conversion of your country. Above all, accept and bear with submission the sufferings that the Lord [the universal, immutable *law* of God] will send you.

"Will you offer sacrifices to God and accept all the sufferings that He will send you in reparation for the many sins which offend His divine majesty [His nature and laws]? Will you suffer to obtain the conversion of sinners and to make amends for all blasphemies and offenses committed against the immaculate heart [the womb or subconscious nature through which the Christ consciousness is born]?"

Speaking time and again through and to children—thus fulfilling the biblical prophecies "A little child shall lead them" and "In order to enter the kingdom of heaven, be as little children"—Mary told fourteen-year-old Mélanie of La Salette:

"If my people will not submit, I shall be forced to let go my son's arm; it is so strong and heavy that I can no longer hold it up. With all your prayers and works you can never make up for all the trouble I have taken on your behalf. . . . If the harvest is ruined it is your fault. Well, children, you will pass on my message to my people." Here she specifically uses "the harvest" as meaning the Latter Days which Jesus prophesied.

During the Franco-Prussian War in 1871, Mary used four children in the little village of Pontmain, France, to prepare one third of its population to witness her message and warnings in the local church through writings formed in large capital letters of gold on a long white scroll that unrolled beneath the feet of the beautiful Lady in apparition.

An invisible hand wrote: "Pray, my children. God will hear you in short time. My son allows himself to be moved." Suddenly the beautiful apparition—which all took to be Mary, Mother of the World—raised her hands, which previously had been stretched out toward the children, and slowly moved her fingers; then looked at them with indescribable tenderness.

Shortly afterwards the Lady's face became clouded with sadness.

She was holding in her hands, before her breast, a red cross bearing a figure of Jesus, also in red, on which there was a white band with the red letters *Jesus Christ*. At the same time she moved her lips and seemed to pray. While they said their night prayers, led by the parish priest, a sort of blue veil came slowly up from the Lady's feet and gradually hid the vision from view. Only the crown remained for a moment, then that disappeared. The apparition had lasted nearly three hours.

Three days later the Prussian army, which was scattered over the region between Mayenne and the eastern part of the district, began to fall back on the Maine-et-Loire and the Sarthe. On January 28th the two warring nations signed an armistice and preliminary peace terms.

Some of the most fully documented appearances of Mary have been those in Garabandal, Spain, from 1961 to 1965. According to the four children who witnessed her apparitions, "Mary is very approachable. She seems to want to close the gap between herself and those on the Earth." This means to those light workers of the present who interpret these as marks of this Latter-Day age that Mary is attempting to break down all barriers between dimensions, to dissolve the veils between the third and fourth dimensional frequencies.

On July 2, 1961, Mary appeared and said: "You must make many sacrifices, do much penance. You must visit the Blessed Sacrament frequently. But first, you must be very good and unless you do this, a punishment will befall you. The cup is already filling and unless you change, the punishment will come."

Conchita of Garabandal reported on January 1, 1965, that if Mary's message through Archangel Michael, which was later delivered to the children on June 18, 1965, were not followed there would be a punishment:

"Our Lady revealed to me what the punishment will consist of. But I can't say what it is, except this: it will be an effect of God's divine intervention, which makes it more fearful than anything imaginable. It will be less terrible for little children to die a natural death than to die of the punishment. The punishment, if it comes, will take place after the miracle."

Archangel Michael delivered this message from Mary to the

entire world: "As my message of the 18th of October has not been complied with, and as it has not been made known to the world, I am telling you that this is the last one I shall give. Previously, the cup was filling up. Now it is brimming over. Many are following the road to perdition and with them they are taking many more souls. We should turn the wrath of God [the divine law of cause and effect] away from us *by our own efforts*. If you ask His forgiveness with a sincere heart, He will pardon you."

Lucy, as sole survivor of the three children of Fatima, in seclusion as a nun, on November 26, 1957, explained: "Three times our Lady has told me we are approaching the Latter Days. We still have time to check heaven's punishment by prayer and penance. There is no material, spiritual, national or international problem that cannot be solved by means of the holy rosary [prayer] and our sacrifices [repentance for our mistakes both as individuals and as a race on Earth]."

After Mary's promised miracle at Fatima, she gave a message to Lucy which was written out and sealed in an envelope deposited in the care of the Bishop of Leiria, but which is now in the Pope's apartments in the Vatican. Only part of it has been revealed.

"Proclaim in my name: a punishment will befall the entire human race. It will not come today or tomorrow but in the second half of the twentieth century. What I revealed at La Salette through the children Mélanie and Maximin I repeat today before you. The human race has sinned and trampled with its feet the gift that was bestowed on it. Nowhere does order reign.

"Satan [sin or error] has reached the very highest places and decides the march of events. He will succeed in introducing himself into and reaching the highest summit of the Church. He will succeed in seducing the minds of great scholars who will invent weapons with which it will be possible to destroy half of mankind in a matter of minutes. He will have powerful nations under his empire and he will lead them to the mass production of these weapons. If mankind does not take steps to stop him, I shall be obliged to let my son's arm [sword of truth] fall.

"And then God will punish man far more severely than when He did so by means of the flood. The great and powerful will perish in the same way as the weak and small. But a time of severe trials will come also for the Church. Cardinal will oppose cardinal and bishop will oppose bishop. Fire and smoke will then fall from the heavens and the waters of the oceans will evaporate; the spray will leap into the sky and everything that is standing will sink. Millions of men will perish by the hour and those who are left alive will envy those who have died."

Reemphasizing her appearances at Fatima, Mary continued with her message of warnings. Appearing to Barbara Reuss in Marienfried, Germany, in the presence of a priest, Reverend Martin Rumpf, and his sister Anna, on May 25, 1946, Mary is reported to have said: "Pray, make sacrifices for sinners. Offer yourselves and your works to the Father through me and put yourselves at my disposal without reserve. . . .

"Pray not so much for external things, weightier things are at stake in these times. Expect no sign or wonders. I shall be active as the powerful Mediatrix in secret. For you I shall procure peace of heart if you will fulfill this request. Then Christ [I Am consciousness] will reign as King of Peace over the nations. Let it be your concern that this wish of mine be made known to the world."

Barbara's third vision on June 25, 1946, records Mary as saying: "I cannot manifest my power to the world in general. I must still hold myself aloof with my children. In secret I shall work marvels in souls till the required number of victims will be filled. Upon you it depends to shorten the days of darkness. This is my message to the world and all people must be informed about it." We believe this refers to the one hundred and forty-four thousand enlightened workers who will spread this message to the world (see Glossary; also, see Mark-Age booklet *The 144,000 Elect*).

Confirming this interpretation, the vision informed Barbara: "A new revelation has been made to the world and they will experience what has been revealed." This refers to the New Age prophecies as coming through Mark-Age and other similar groups around the globe. Mary said to Barbara that the details need not be remembered, but that people do what she has requested and follow the will of the Father.

When Barbara begged for an outward sign to prove these visions, Mary only replied: "I have already given many signs and spoken often to the world but people have not taken them seriously. On account of these outward signs the greater multitude do not even grasp the essential things. Outward signs only succeed in annoying many who do not draw the necessary conclusions from them. My children must praise and love and thank the Eternal more. He has created everyone for His glory. Many prayers should be offered for sinners."

MIRACLES THROUGH MARY

Mary's authenticated appearances always have been accompanied by acts of grace, love and charity. Man calls these miracles, but really they are events beyond our physically known and accepted laws of science. So, we have witnessed healings, teachings, prophecies, levitations, movements and lights in the skies, and a general upliftment and dedication to spiritual life.

The Coptic religious weekly *Watani* in Egypt carried accounts from 1968 through 1971 of some of the most outstanding cures and miracles that were associated with Mary's apparitions in the church of Zeitun, near Cairo.

The grotto at Lourdes, which had been perfectly dry when Bernadette was told to dig a hole in the ground, now furnishes thirty-three thousand gallons of water a day. Sixty-five cures have been authenticated since 1858. This means they have passed the scrutiny and post-examinations of medical doctors and Church authorities. Millions of people have visited there to be spiritually inspired and uplifted.

At Garabandal the spiritual demonstrations as a result of Mary's appearances included: levitations by the children, miraculous healings from objects which Mary either touched or kissed, mental telepathy, prophecy, trances of a high spiritual nature, and communication with those who have passed beyond the physical.

Also in 1962, seventy-nine frames of movie film showed the child Conchita, with her head tilted back, receiving Holy Communion from Archangel Michael. The host appeared as a hazy white substance which increased in size and density upon her tongue. Hundreds of people witnessed this event despite attempts to stop it. Numerous physicians examined the children during their ecstasies and afterward, confirming these events to be supernatural in origin.

Jesus channeled through me on May 3, 1961: "The Fatima message refers to communication with other planets and life in other spheres. It also refers to changes that must take place on this Earth before the fourth dimension can be fully operative." The fourth dimension is the higher frequency vibration at which all will be functioning.

Thus it was that Mary, preparing the masses for this great change in frequency vibration, predicted to the children of Fatima on July 13, 1917: "In October I shall work a great miracle so that everyone will believe you."

On the appointed date between 12:05 and 12:15 P.M., seventy thousand pilgrims gathered in a forbidding rainstorm to await the miracle. Suddenly the rain stopped. In scarcely a minute the clouds dispersed. The sun appeared. But it was not golden; rather, it was a silver disc. It seemed to be surrounded by another disc whose color the spectators could not state, beyond saying that it was dazzling, though they acknowledged that this effect might have been due for the moment to the sudden appearance of the sun in a sky which had been so overcast.

The sun remained motionless for an instant and then, as abruptly as it had appeared, began to tremble. It almost looked as if it were shaking itself. It stopped trembling and then began to spin around, shooting out on all sides rays of light which changed color. These rays were, in turn, red, blue, violet and green. They colored the spectators' faces. The sun stopped spinning and stood still in the heavens; then it began to spin around, again throwing out colored rays of even greater brilliance. It then stopped spinning for the second time.

A moment passed and then the spectators received the impression that the sun detached itself from the sky. Literally, it seemed to jump in space. It zigzagged about from east to west and then, as if quite eccentric, it appeared to fall from the sky, plunging towards the Earth and giving out unbearable heat.

The sun or the disc came to rest for a third time. Then it zigzagged its way up into the sky and back to its original place. The sky remained clear, with no sign of clouds. The spectators suddenly realized that their clothes, which had been soaked and were clinging to their bodies from the storm, were dry.

The descriptions of the phenomenon comply with experiences of UFO or extraterrestrial spacecraft sightings throughout the world. One atheist reporter on the scene said, "It looked like a dull silvery plaque, as if an eclipse."

No observatory in the world recorded anything in the least resembling a solar disturbance. But the phenomena were observed outside the Cova by one who was six and a quarter miles from Fatima and another who observed it thirty-one miles away.

SECRETS OF THINGS TO COME

In spite of all these messages, pilgrimages of millions, prayers, miracles and other demonstrations, Mary and Jesus have issued a number of secrets to those on whom they have bestowed visits.

Mary, channeling through me on November 7, 1962, said: "I am guiding and controlling these beings or individuals who have dedicated themselves to the mother or the soul aspect, the subconscious or womb of life, as it is manifesting for the rest of the realm or the race of mankind upon the Earth. Be then cognizant of these urgings and these yearnings from the soul within you."

On February 20, 1858, Bernadette Soubirous was given a secret prayer by the Lady, which was not part of the catechism, and the child was made to promise never to reveal the words to anyone. Until her death from tuberculosis at thirty-six, Bernadette kept her promise and refused even her priests when they questioned her about the prayer.

Conchita at Garabandal has said: "The Virgin told me on January 1, 1965, that it [the secret she is not permitted to speak of] will be visible to everybody everywhere. It will be a direct work of God and will take place before the great miracle. I do not know whether people will die because of it. They could only die from the shock of seeing it. . . .

"It will be on the order of a phenomenon similar to fire or light. It will be seen first in the sky. It will be seen by all. Then, it will be present everywhere and will be felt by all, no matter where one would be at the time. It will be as if our sins will be revealed to us. I do not know how long it will last, but within ten minutes after its start the entire world would be in terror."

This is only the warning, and is meant to purify the world in order for it to receive the great miracle. Conchita, who is only one of four girls who saw Mary at Garabandal, has said: "The Virgin told only me about the miracle. She forbade me to say what it will consist of. I cannot reveal the date, either, until eight days beforehand.

"What I am allowed to say is that it will coincide with an event in the Church and with the feast of a saint who is a martyr of the holy Eucharist. It will be at half-past eight on a Thursday evening. It will be visible to everyone in the village and on the surrounding mountainsides. The sick who are present will be cured and the incredulous will believe. It will be the greatest miracle that Jesus has ever worked for the world.

CHILDREN OF GARABANDAL
Ecstatic trance was one response of the children who witnessed the apparitions of the Blessed Mary, 1961–1965

"There will not remain the slightest doubt that it comes from God and is for the good of mankind. In the pine grove [at Garabandal] a sign of the miracle will be left at that spot forever as proof. It will be possible to film and televise the whole thing. But the sign cannot be touched. It will be recognized as a thing not of this world and that it comes from God."

Further cleansings also are part of the Garabandal message through Conchita. "The punishment is conditioned to whether or not mankind heeds the Blessed Virgin's messages and the miracle. If the punishment does take place, then I know what it will consist of, because Mary told me. What is more, I have seen it. What I can assure you is that if it comes it is far worse than if we were enveloped in fire, worse than if we had fire above us and fire beneath. I do not know how long a time will elapse after the miracle before God sends it."

Conchita also had an experience with Jesus on December 8, 1964. She wrote it down for a priest who asked her to do so.

Conchita: Why is the miracle coming? To convert people?

Jesus: To convert the whole world.

Conchita: Will Russia be converted?

Jesus: She also will be converted and thus everybody will love our hearts.

Conchita: Will the punishment come after that? (No answer.) Why have you come to my poor, undeserving heart?

Jesus: I have not come for your sake, I have come for everybody's sake.

Conchita: Is the miracle going to happen as if I were the only one to have seen the Blessed Virgin?

Jesus: For your sacrifices, your forbearance, I am allowing you to be the intercessor to work the miracle.

Conchita: Would it not be better if it were all of us, or otherwise if you did not make any of us the intercessor?

Jesus: No.

Conchita: Will I die soon?

Jesus: You will have to be on Earth to help the world.

Conchita: I am worthless. I shall not be able to help at all.

Jesus: By your prayers and sufferings you will help the world.

Conchita: When people go to heaven, do they go dead?

Jesus: People never die.

Conchita: But I thought we did not go to heaven until we were resurrected. Is St. Peter at the gates of heaven to receive us?

Jesus: No. . . . Pray hard for the priests so that they may be saintly and do their duty and make others better, that they may make me known to those who do not know me, and that they may make me loved by those who know me but do not love me.

&

Repeatedly the messages from the spiritual Hierarchy through me had pointed out 1972 as the key turning point in alerting all mankind that we are in the Latter Days. That year marked the acceleration of the mass educational program through I Am Nation citizens everywhere, to be followed by further spiritual demonstrations, beginning in the mid-1980s, that would prepare all on the planet for the Second Coming.

Therefore, this final message by Jacinta of Fatima, sent to Pope Pius XII in 1954 by Mother Godinho, who recorded it as the child lay dying, gave this pertinent warning:

"Mary told Jacinta to prepare for the year 1972 because the sins of impurity and vanity and of excessive luxury would bring upon the world such punishments that they will cause much suffering to the Holy Father. The triumph of Our Lord would yet come. But there would first be many tears because the will of God is not being fulfilled in the world. . . .

"There is a secret of heaven and another one of Earth. The latter is terrifying. It will seem as though it were already the end of the world. In this cataclysm everything will be separated from the sky, which will turn white as snow."

All hear, then, Jesus—with Mary coming in advance, full of pregnant help and advice—to prepare this planet and all mankind on it for the Second Coming around the year 2000.

SPIRITUAL
SPACE PROGRAM

After twenty years of investigating UFOs or Unidentified Flying Objects, in the 1960s the U.S. Air Force prepared a textbook for its cadets including a fourteen-page chapter devoted exclusively to this subject. The book warned that scientific studies of the UFO mystery had so far been based on man's present limited knowledge of physics and this present knowledge may not apply to UFOs.

The textbook, now out of print, reads: "One thing that must be guarded against in any such study is the trap of implicitly assuming that our knowledge of physics (or any other branch of science) is complete. We should not deny the possibility of alien control of UFOs on the basis of preconceived notions."

The textbook lists three possible reasons why we may be visited from beings of other planets or realms. It is the third one that is of most interest and value to those who understand the hierarchal plan and program now in effect upon Earth. Further it indicates that the Air Force has seriously pondered the true spiritual material that has been channeled and disseminated on Earth since the late 1940s.

"(1) We may be the object of intensive sociological and psychological study. In such studies you usually avoid disturbing the test subjects' environment.

"(2) You do not contact a colony of ants—and humans may seem that way to any aliens (variation: a zoo is fun to visit, but you don't contact the lizards).

"(3) Such contact may have already taken place secretly, and may have taken place on a different plane of awareness—and we are not yet sensitive to communications on such a plane."

EARTHMAN ON THE MOON — AND BEYOND

Of the almost six billion souls incarnated on Earth now, most of those aware of Earthman's space program as developed by the USA, Russia (former Soviet Union), and other nations, have wondered of the purpose and value of such a gigantic effort. With so many problems facing humankind, it is only natural a large segment of the population should be concerned about this vast expenditure of funds, energy, scientific research, and resources. Is it all worth it? they ask. Here is the spiritual answer to this issue, based on information I have received since 1958 from those concerned with spiritual government; and which we have published since 1960, particularly in our textbook *Visitors From Other Planets.*

God—or Spirit or Creative Energy or Divine Mind—is the Source and Creator of all that eternally exists. Mankind collectively is the Son of God and as such also eternally exists, not only as a kingdom but as individuals. The Son of God or body of mankind inhabits all realms of God's universes. Mankind evolves throughout his eternal existence, to become and to function as a cocreator with God. In this spiritual evolvement he progresses through a vast number of schools and rooms in our Father's many mansions.

Within our solar system there are the physical planets, each with its own astral planes, with the etheric or spiritual realm common to all the planets. Each planet and each astral plane represents a different level of attainment, the etheric being the highest for man. When we earn a passing grade we advance to a higher plane or planet. When we fail we must stay in the same schoolroom, be it the physical planet or its astral planes, until we are qualified to pass.

GRADUATION TIME

It is graduation time for the race of man assigned to the Earth planet and its astral planes. All here are being given the opportunity to rise from the mortal to the divine. Those who earnestly seek to pass and to go on with their spiritual evolvement will make the greatest advances yet in their soul history. Those who do not wish to advance into the next level of evolvement will be taken out of the solar system in which they have evolved with others for eons of time. Those who do make the grade will come back to Earth in the Golden Age or will evolve to higher planes and planets.

No one originated on Earth and no one will end here. Man as a species came from a higher state of evolution, became enmeshed in the third dimension of materiality and consciousness, and has been making his way back to his true spiritual status (see our text-books *Evolution of Man* and *Angels and Man*). Many have made it already and have gone on to live in physical worlds of the fourth through the eighth dimensions or ranges of frequency vibration in this solar system, or to live even beyond this system. These ranges of physical expressions are beyond the five physical senses and instruments of Earthman today; our space probes to other planets cannot detect, as yet, these frequencies. Spirit does not duplicate schools, lessons and manners of expression.

Normally there are communication and travel between the various planets and planes within the solar system. Man on Earth partook of this interdimensional and interplanetary intercourse until as recently as the civilization of Atlantis, some twelve to fifteen thousand years ago. But man then lost his spiritual contact with God and his fellowmen of this and other worlds, seeking segregation rather than integration into the Federation of Planets in this solar system. The spiritual government or Hierarchal Board of this solar system had no choice but to draw the veil over Earthman's consciousness to such an extent that even awareness of life beyond the physical one on Earth has been hidden, except to spiritually sensitive souls who help to give us insight into our higher powers: ESP = Elementary Spiritual Powers.

Now the time has come for Earth and all on it to be raised into a higher, the fourth, dimension or range of frequency vibration. To aid in this process, many of higher realms have been incarnating on Earth. Others have come via mental communication, projection of their bodies and in the spacecraft called flying saucers or UFOs by man of Earth. Performing a myriad of purposes and accomplishing goals beyond human imagination, these visitors from other planets and planes have been helping prepare the way for Earthman to rejoin the race of man throughout this solar system.

MAKING MAN SPACE CONSCIOUS

To be effective, this has had to be a multifaceted spiritual project, called the hierarchal or Mark Age plan and program. A vital phase of this project has been to make Earthman space conscious. This has been done in part by millions having witnessed or having believed the demonstrations in the skies performed via the spacecraft of our sisters and brothers of other realms, accomplishing feats Earth science cannot duplicate. But there has been far more aid of a more subtle nature through mental projection of thoughts to Earthman concerning those scientific principles which have enabled him to go to the moon in person and throughout the solar system by probe.

So, the goal of making Earthman space conscious has been achieved. He knows space travel is possible. This has enabled him to entertain the possibility or probability or certainty that life must exist elsewhere, be it as we know it on Earth or in other forms. This now has opened the way for man of other worlds to appear openly on Earth and to be accepted as visitors from other planets. This then will permit our fellowmen of higher evolvement to explain the Federation of Planets to which all mankind in this solar system now belongs, except those of Earth.

MAN'S SPIRITUAL HERITAGE

Through the teachings, demonstrations and assistance of our sisters and brothers from other realms, we of Earth will learn again of our spiritual nature, heritage, talents, powers, purposes, our past and future. We will understand the present crisis, and yet this golden opportunity, as concerns our individual and planetary graduation into a higher physical and spiritual evolvement, and we shall be inspired to work together to achieve that purpose. Then truly will the way in space become the way in Spirit for man of Earth.

This, then, is the real purpose behind God's guidance of man in the Earth space program, an integral part of the hierarchal space program, which itself is but a part of the vast Hierarchal Board program which has been in effect for nearly twenty-six thousand years to lift man of Earth to his rightful position in this solar system. Thus was the race into space literally a race toward destiny, for there has been but little margin of time remaining for this transmutation of Earth and all on it before the entire solar system enters a new level of manifestation and evolution.

Yes, the Earth space program, actually instituted by God and the Hierarchal Board, has been beyond realization of value in material terms, for it has opened the door to a new dimension, to man's spiritual awakening. No matter now that the awakening could have been accomplished eons ago or could have been done in better ways. For it has been a crash program necessitated by the solar system's needs, and thus had to be accomplished by the end of this twentieth century in the best and fastest manner possible. It has been accomplished, through the grace and guidance of God and the assistance of untold billions from other worlds.

This is the Mark Age or Latter-Day period, known also as the War of Armageddon. In the 1960s, the two nations engaged in the race to the moon were the USA, founded and declared to be under God, and the USSR (Soviet Union), then an avowed atheistic government. Thus it was a battle of the Christ versus the anti-Christ forces, or of those who believed in the brotherhood of man under God and those who did not. The spiritually dedicated nation won.

But would Earthman have achieved the goal and have become space conscious from this planet without overt outside intervention if there had not been such a race or battle? And not all the citizens of the USA could be categorized in the Christ forces, nor all those of the USSR as of the anti-Christ. All of us are children of God, loved equally and dearly by our Creator. Thus all have benefited and have participated, even in those nations not directly involved. But the USA is a nation developed by God and the Hierarchal Board to become the New JerUSAlem, a spiritual government on the Earth in the New Age now beginning.

APOLLO 11 MOON MISSION

Those who have been aware of the hierarchal program have seen much significance and evidence of divine direction, guidance and protection in the Earth space program of the USA. As prelude to the Apollo missions, consider that there were seven original astronauts. Seven is a spiritually significant number in all creation. It is especially significant now in that it represents the seventh step of mankind and the rending of the seven phases of the last or seventh veil that separates man from his spiritual awareness.* The first sub-orbital flight by the USA was in a capsule named *Freedom Seven.*

There were the Mercury, Gemini and Apollo series of flights. Mercury is a legendary bearer of messages or news, or a conductor of travelers: those of higher realms coming to aid man, or man's own spiritual Self calling upon the mortal self to awaken and to rise. Gemini is the sign of the twin: man of other realms and man of Earth, or spiritual Self and mortal self. Apollo is the name of the sun god: the son of man becoming the son of God. The Saturn rocket lifted the Apollo craft: Saturn is the seat of the Saturnian Council, the Council of Seven that spiritually rules this solar system.

Apollo 11 spacecraft, the *Columbia,* named for Christopher Columbus, and the *Eagle* lunar module, making one think of the New Testament's prophecies of the Second Coming, were named by President Richard Nixon, who was a worker on the Sixth Ray of Transmutation under Chohan St. Germain. The present activity of St. Germain is as Dr. Hannibal, in charge from the etheric realm of the Western Hemisphere for the hierarchal space program, who had been Christopher Columbus and whose present spacecraft of city size is #1235, which is a Unit #11 craft.

The Apollo 11 moon mission from July 16 to 24, 1969, to land Earthman on the moon was one of the major spiritual events on the physical plane to help raise man into the fourth dimension, both physically and in consciousness. For the entire month of July, I was led to be in spiritual retreat away from Mark-Age headquarters (at that time in Miami, Florida), but nearby. Some of my high Self or Nada Self activities in the light body were observed by associates at headquarters and elsewhere. I present these experiences pertaining to the Apollo 11 mission so that all can appreciate fully this spiritually directed hierarchal program.

While watching the liftoff of Apollo 11 on July 16th, I experi-

---

* At this turn of the century, we are rending the seventh and final phase of the seventh veil that separates us from the higher, I Am consciousness. It is expected to be completed around 2003.

enced a flow of thoughts concerning the spiritual significance of the names and locations involved in the U.S. space program, similar to those already related. Part of my meditation was in connection with the concurrent ripping of the third phase of the seventh veil from mass consciousness. That phase began in April 1968 and extended to spring 1970, after which time man of Earth increasingly became aware of the hierarchal program.

During the afternoon of July 16th, while in my light body, as Nada of the Hierarchal Board, I entered the Apollo 11 craft and spoke silently to astronauts Armstrong, Aldrin and Collins: "Lift up all men. Rip the veil. Power and love are united." Power is the First Ray aspect or function of divine will and power, the first step for man in his spiritual awakening: bowing to the will of God so as to be able to use the power of God. Love is a Seventh Ray aspect or function of divine love and peace, the final or rest step for man in his spiritual awakening or moving into a new level.

That Wednesday evening of July 16th during a meditation at 7:45 P.M. I met Sananda, and some of his disciples from his last Earth incarnation as Christ Jesus of Nazareth, in an astral realm. I watched them descend from the etheric realm. Sananda embraced me and asked why I had called him. I replied, "We need a sign, an outer sign; not for myself, but a sign that would satisfy all mankind as to your influence and presence in this day and age."

"No single proof would satisfy all men," Sananda answered.

"For me it would make no difference," I insisted. "But the peoples of Earth need something they cannot explain, regardless of whether or not they can accept it for what it is. And we, the program workers whom you have selected on the Earth, need something, also, to work with."

"You will have a sign of this visit. You have my word. It will be there and you will know it," Sananda/Jesus promised.

My light body then descended over my physical body like a bell over a clapper. I was in two bodies, yet I could operate in both simultaneously. Once again I visited the Apollo 11 crew and from their craft projected golden rays to Earth, bathing it in divine love in preparation for the rending of the third phase of the last veil, stating, "And the third step in the final rending of the seventh veil of mystery for man of Earth shall be!"

109

Two hours later I was watching a movie on television, when it was interrupted by a nonscheduled videotape broadcast from the Apollo mooncraft. At 8:00 P.M. (fifteen minutes after my contact with Sananda) the crew unexpectedly decided to broadcast pictures of the Earth from sixty thousand miles away. Unmistakably, I saw the face of Jesus stamped over the Earth exactly as he had appeared to me just prior to the Apollo transmission. This was his sign. In a subtle, even humorous, way he had demonstrated his reply that all would *not* know or accept the same sign which all could see.

On the second day of the flight, July 17th, I channeled through my physical body the light or understanding of God to all men of Earth. This was a channeling of higher spiritual energies being reinstated to Earth for the first time since Atlantis, when I as Yolanda, high priestess of the Sun Temple near what is now Miami, Florida, had helped the Hierarchal Board withdraw them from use by man of Earth. This reinstatement was being done for the rending of the third phase of the seventh veil.

During the third and fourth days of the voyage of Apollo 11, I spent all my time and energy spiritually preparing the astronauts. My body, as an instrument for the channeling of this higher or hieronic energy, was used to synchronize their bodies to the new frequency vibration they would experience in going out of the third dimensional environment of Earth. It is doubtful the astronauts consciously would have known anything of this activity, other than an upliftment in contemplation or meditation or in some dream episode. Nevertheless it was effected and so must be recorded for the race record.

At the end of this energy transmission on the fourth day I was told mentally that I would receive confirmation, of the ability of the moonwalkers to receive my projections, by reading the profile on Armstrong in *Life* magazine for July 4, 1969. The opening paragraph contains: "When Neil Armstrong was a small boy, he had a recurrent dream: he could, by holding his breath, hover over the ground. Nothing much ever happened—he neither flew nor fell, just hovered." In another article I read, Armstrong is quoted as having confided to a friend after a series of mishaps, "I should be dead. But I guess God has something else for me to do in my life."

From 11:00 P.M. on Sunday, July 20th through Monday, July

21st, when astronauts Armstrong and Aldrin were physically on the moon, I was watching it on television with Mark. I was aware of an electromagnetic beam from Dr. Hannibal, aboard his own spacecraft headquarters aiding the *Eagle*'s activities. This beam also was a hieronic transmission for helping to change the frequency vibration of the two astronauts, as representatives of all Earthmen and as the matrix for the race's physical form now ready to go from third dimensional frequency into the fourth dimension.

As soon as they had reentered their spacecraft after the historic moonwalk, Dr. Hannibal told me via mental telepathic communication: "You were the focal point on Earth for transmitting the change in frequency for third dimensional frequency form of human bodies. All men on Earth will notice some change in their bodies, though this may come to their attention very gradually."

On the seventh day, Katoomi/Archangel Michael, titular head of the Hierarchal Board, contacted me to relay that at the splashdown of the Apollo 11 crew the next day, July 24th, I would be released from my special assignment: "Your special attention, prayers and light-body projections, as well as those of all Mark-Age associates who are in proper spiritual understanding of this mission, helped raise the astronauts sufficiently in vibration and spiritual consciousness so they had a deeper and more spiritual appreciation of what they have accomplished for all mankind. There has been a rise in race consciousness.

"From this point onward the light workers on Earth will have better contact with their fellowmen. But it has been necessary for us to use channels and broadcasting units of light through physical vessels such as yourself on the Earth plane itself to do this work. Regardless of whether or not the program workers personally feel they have been influential in this task, they have been necessary and a prerequisite to our functions and goals. You have completed your task. The men who have been instruments for us shall be returned to you on Earth safe and well."

On January 9, 1971, Dr. Hannibal channeled this through me, at NASA in Houston with Mark: "[Earthman] actually is breaking the barriers of his physical environment and body when he goes out into space. This is absolutely necessary for him to do in his physical body. It is not so important that he do it by mechanical means or through computer services, such as being demonstrated by other areas and other nations in their explorations into space.

"It is good, it is fine to do these things via mechanics. But it is absolutely essential, in these Latter Days and in his ability to lift himself beyond his own physical body and his own limited consciousness of mortal being, that he do it in the physical sense of the word. It is so very important that your astronauts be seen and that it be known unto all men that all men have created and have cracked the environment beyond Earth and have gone beyond that which is keeping them in lower areas of experience and experiment. They have created forms by which they can reach out beyond that which has them chained in the Earth."

ONGOING TRANSFORMATIONS

As illustrated above, light workers play an important role in assisting the Hierarchal Board to raise the frequency vibration of Earth via humanity's representatives who travel into space. Since the Apollo missions, behind-the-scenes spiritual works have continued, for instance, during the missions of the U.S. *Skylab* and space shuttle programs, and Russia's *Salyut* and *Mir* space stations.

Earthman's presence in space has become commonplace. Having taken our initial baby steps as a spacefaring civilization, we also have slowly conditioned ourselves for more overt contact with visitors from other planets, thereby eventually to rejoin the Federation of Planets. Even our mechanical probes to the other planets of our solar system, as well as discoveries provided by the Hubble Space Telescope, have served our ongoing awakening as cosmic citizens.

Though only a relative handful of Earthlings have traveled into space, we all have benefited. All of us, not just the space explorers, have been subtly transformed in consciousness. Indeed, space-age literature is replete with testimonials to the life-changing, transformative experience of physical space travel—written by the astronauts and cosmonauts themselves. Perhaps the best known of these is the account of astronaut Dr. Edgar Mitchell, who walked on the moon in February 1971 during the mission of Apollo 14.

Mitchell, who now works to integrate science with spirituality, recounts his transformation in his autobiography, *The Way of the*

Explorer: An Apollo Astronaut's Journey Through the Material and Mystical Worlds (G.P. Putnam's Sons, New York, 1996). Unbeknownst to NASA officials at the time, he conducted ESP experiments with telepathy during his lunar voyage, with the collaboration of several non-NASA colleagues. The results of these experiments, later published in the *Journal of Parapsychology,* proved statistically significant.

Now, what also is of great interest is the profound epiphany, or cosmic revelation, that Astronaut Mitchell experienced on the return flight of Apollo 14. He subsequently came to understand this life-changing episode as an experience of what the Hindus call *samadhi,* an intimate awareness of

EDGAR MITCHELL
On the moon, 1971

one's interconnectedness with the "All That Is." In our parlance, we can liken this to a light-body overshadowing, an expansion of cosmic consciousness, a union with the Godhead.

In his book, Mitchell relays that, once he had left the moon and was back aboard the command module, most of his responsibilities were completed. "I had time to relax in weightlessness," he writes, "and contemplate that blue jewel-like home planet suspended in the velvety blackness from which we had come. What I saw out the window was all I had ever known, all I had ever loved and hated, longed for, all that I once thought had ever been and ever would be. It was all there suspended in the cosmos on that fragile little sphere. I experienced a grand epiphany accompanied by exhilaration. . . . From that moment, my life was irrevocably altered.

"What I experienced during that three-day trip home was nothing short of an overwhelming sense of universal *connectedness.* I actually felt what has been described as an ecstasy of unity. It occurred to me that the molecules of my body and the molecules of the spacecraft itself were manufactured long ago in the furnace of one of the ancient stars that burned in the heavens about me. And there was the sense that our presence as space travelers, and the existence of the universe itself, was not accidental but that there was an intelligent process at work. I perceived the universe as in some way conscious. The thought was so large it seemed at the time inexpressible."

Later, Mitchell elaborates: "As I looked beyond the Earth itself to the magnificence of the larger scene, there was a startling recognition that the nature of the universe was not as I had been taught. My understanding of the separate distinctness and the relative independence of movement of those cosmic bodies was shattered. There was an upwelling of fresh insight coupled with a feeling of ubiquitous harmony—a sense of interconnectedness with the celestial bodies surrounding our spacecraft. . . . I not only *saw* the connectedness, I *felt* it and experienced it sentiently. I was overwhelmed with the sensation of physically and mentally extending out into the cosmos. The restraints and boundaries of flesh and bone fell away."

Once he returned to Earth, Mitchell avidly pursued studies of esoteric, mystical philosophy and began to correlate his experiences with high-frontier scientific research. He came to view himself as a modern-day shaman: "My life's purpose, I now see, has been to reveal and interpret information, first in outer space, and now in inner space." His experience as a scientist-astronaut, plus his subsequent explorations of mysticism, give Dr. Mitchell a particular insight into the integration of science and spirituality.

In early 1973, after he left the astronaut corps, he formed a nonprofit research and educational organization, the Institute of Noetic Sciences, which still publishes a variety of materials highlighting their pursuits.* For example, the institute investigated and documented the legitimate paranormal powers of world-renowned Israeli psychic, metal bender, and UFO contactee, Uri Geller.

The transformation of Edgar Mitchell, and of many of the other space explorers, shows the effectiveness of interdimensional coordination in the spiritual space program. Astronauts, light workers, interplanetary visitors—together we are transforming planet Earth, preparing all life for entrance into the Golden Age of Aquarius.

---

* Institute of Noetic Sciences, 475 Gate Five Road, Suite 300, Sausalito, CA 94965. Phone 1-800-383-1394. Visit their website at: http://www.noetic.org.

SPIRITUAL RELATIONSHIP OF MAN & ANIMALS

IN THE BEGINNING

God made the wild animals according to their kinds, the livestock according to their kinds, and all the creatures that move along the ground according to their kinds. And God saw that it was good.

Then God said, "Let us make man in our image, in our likeness, and let them rule over the fish of the sea and the birds of the air, over the livestock, over all the Earth, and over all the creatures that move along the ground." – Genesis 1:25–26

Metaphysically we know that the words *image* and *likeness* mean "nature." And when the Bible says that we are made in the image and likeness of God our Creator, it refers to the fact that the source of our being is of the same nature. We are made of Spirit, since God our Creator is Spirit. So, from this instruction we must understand that the Bible tells us we have dominion over forms that are of lesser evolution and consciousness than we, who are like and have the powers of the Creator.

Also, we are told in Genesis that we are to name the animals. *Name* means "nature of." Therefore, it means we are to understand and to work with the nature that each species represents in the evolutionary progress of third dimensional or physical form on this particular planet.

The channelings through me are replete with references to our relationship with the animal kingdom and to our responsibilities as sons and daughters of God to those species.*

"The balance between every kingdom—your animal, mineral and vegetable kingdoms—is very delicately attuned to one another for

---

* See especially the Mark-Age textbooks *Evolution of Man* and *Angels and Man.*

115

certain facets of creation. Not only on their physical dimension but also in their other bodies or properties are they so balanced. There are astral vibrations of every single form you know in your Earth planet. And there are many forms which affect the Earth or physical, third dimension as you know it which are never appearing in a physical form."

—John Mark; March 14, 1962

"Seven steps are required to bring about manifested form. Seven words or ideas are involved. . . . This is repeated on every level of creation and in every step of evolution.

"It begins on the realms and in the consciousness of those that are the elohim, out of the Godhead. It is entrusted into the hands of the angelic, celestial planes, whereby all the elements are in divine control and creative force. It is held under the guardianship of the celestial realm until the special creation of God, the Son, the race of man, can comprehend that service or area of performance. Under the children of God all lesser forms of creation which are in the process of evolution, the animal and the vegetable and the mineral kingdoms, are held in balance and in supervision."

—Jesus; March 19, 1969

It becomes obvious in understanding these divine revelations in the scriptures of all ages and places, including those of the present day which are coming to the channels of this new era, that man was created to have supervision and governance over the lesser kingdoms when he learns his proper relationship in the Godhead.

Man is the Son of God—that is, the race of man is—and in our evolving consciousness we come to understand and to use these powers which are inherent in us. It is the purpose of the Mark Age period and program to teach and to demonstrate this new level of consciousness and to bring about a concerted, unified desire and ability to bring all other kingdoms on the planet and throughout the solar system into their proper relationships.

"Out of this living God you are life and experience life, and give life unto others as well. You are the life-giving substance to those who are of a lesser kingdom. Not that you of yourselves create these lesser kingdoms, but by giving them a purpose in their creation, by

116

being part of their purpose in creation, you are to them as gods; as we [angelic realm], in many cases, seem to you to be gods before the throne of God. . . .

"Therefore, you must learn to be as their [animal, vegetable, mineral kingdoms] guides in a proper way and to be their way showers in a very high and spiritual manner. For, of them Spirit also is the essence and is the whole and the total sense of triune creation.

"Out of this you must become more spiritualized yourselves. In seeking this unification and this overseership with them, you will gain your own higher evolution and truth and principle. For from them came the being and the need to sustain the life form through which you yourselves would have a form and an existence in this particular dimension. . . .

"They are like the soul substance or record keeper of your own experiences. From out of all these substances and elements you reap that which you sowed into their consciousness, and are experiencing the very playback of your own words or thoughts."

– Archangel Uriel; August 17, 1970

EVOLUTION

Although the spiritually minded know they are part of all creation, and all creation is part of them, it has been recorded and taught by all of the highest teachers of spiritual understanding that man, animal, mineral, vegetable, angelic kingdoms are separate and individual species which have their own evolutionary patterns and purposes.

It has been emphasized through my channelings that there is no crossing over, no evolving out of one lower form into a higher form. Each species and realm has its own function and purpose. Again and again it has been emphasized that they must know each other, experience each other, love one another. But they do not incarnate in the various patterns and experiences of the others' forms.

"At first, when this planet was created in all of its glory and beauty with a series of elements quite unlike any other dimension within this solar system, the various sons or lights were attracted to the elements and entered into the elements and experienced life form through them. This is not the same as saying man evolved up

117

out of the elements. But because man did experience through these elements and participated in these elements, he has a race memory of being inside, or part of or participating in, the very elements of which his physical form is made up. It is out of this that he must now evolve. . . .

"Many entered into . . . animal forms in the levels of their creation from the fish through the bird and through the crawling and walking creatures of this planet. But that does not mean the souls or the children of God, the light or elohim, participated in an incarnation through these things. Because mankind is an etheric or spiritual life and light he can participate in any kind of form or matter for a length of time, depending on his ability to sustain intelligence and control over that. Many can do it for an hour or two, and some even have been able to do it for weeks at a time."

– Nada; August 16, 1970

Other channels of this advanced era likewise have received the same guidance and instruction from their mentors on the etheric and angelic realms of this solar system.

The teacher Ban-dhu transmitted the following thoughts through Illiana of the New Age Teachings in Brookfield, Massachusetts:

"There are many of Earth who believe in all sincerity that the animal soul's evolvement eventually causes it to be reborn into a human form. We do not agree with this. As we said to you in other talks: plant souls, animal souls, human souls always evolve through rebirth in their own kind. . . .

"When a soul leaves the animal body, it travels in astral planes for a period of time, learning and preparing, much as your souls do and often in the same spheres. It is not unusual for the human soul to be reunited with his animal soul friend upon transition. The animal soul progresses and is reborn. It has its karma also. As its progress develops, it travels to different planes of higher elevation, just as you humans do.

"The animal souls' cycle of rebirth follows much the same pattern that your souls do. Again remember that universal law *is,* and is for all forms of life. There is not one law for one form and another law for another form. All exist under the same cosmic, universal laws and are subject to the same causes and effects."

118

The channels of the Axminster Group in Devonshire, England, also have received in conscious, mental telepathic communication proper spiritual relationship between man and the animal kingdoms. In a question-and-answer session one of the group asked, "Has the essence of consciousness, as used by the Creative Force to create man, been evolved through the animal, vegetable and mineral kingdoms through its own evolution of experience?"

The answer received through their channel Beta was: "The two branches of creation are separate, created upon different wavelengths of vibration. One did not evolve out of the other. Yet, going back to the Prime Source, *all was.* So, at one time all did stem from the same Source. But for the purpose of creation upon this planet it was achieved upon different wavelengths of vibration."

In the out-of-print series *Mark-Age Broadcasts,* which were questions and answers from media appearances of Mark and me in the 1960s, we have this information, based on a question asked of Mark:

"Yes, animals grow through their own evolution, but only within their own kingdom. There are races and creations of animals in the animal kingdom which have evolved far beyond what most men on Earth can comprehend. They have intelligence, can communicate not only with their own species but with men and other kingdoms, and evolve consciously in orderly and planned manner. Some of them guide the animal race on Earth and are helping prepare it for a higher level of evolvement and expression with new and improved species in the fourth dimension to which the Earth and all on it are being raised now."

MAN'S RESPONSIBILITIES TO ANIMALS

As our spiritual Self awakens more and more in these Latter Days, preparing for the Aquarian Age to come, we will learn our proper relationships to the animal kingdom. This is unfolding now and is part of the I Am Nation's University of Life teachings. For the University of Life is the universal schoolroom for understanding and applying the proper laws of the universe to living on whatever sphere or planet, plane or dimension we are in.

Hierarchal instructions for the University of Life given through me include the following:

"So much of your mass educational program is to involve the informing of the nations about the animal, mineral and vegetable kingdoms. This is something the light workers have been alerted to and have been instructed about, to a small and minor degree, up until this approximate date and proclamation. However, much more is to be learned and to be discerned by those who come into the light-body formation.

"It is the work of the light body, or the etheric mastership of the sons of man, to bring about a more equalized relationship between all life forms with which they share in planetary existence. As a matter of fact, it is so on all dimensions, planes and planets that there are other and varied life forms.

"You have come in contact with these varied life forms in astral projections, in dreams and meditative states. But you have not understood always what they signified, and unfortunately too often you have interpreted them to be varied levels of consciousness of the race of man himself. . . .

"There are so many varied life forms and functions and purposes for Life Force Itself to express in balancing the elements throughout all eternity that you have yet to comprehend all the intricate details of it. This is why this educational program [University of Life] is so extremely important. It is to inform you about this precisely. You will be informed correctly and will perform your function if you but will allow the higher guidance to supersede the lower experience and the fears which you have transposed into the life as you live it upon the Earth in the present time and age of *now.*"

— Sananda; April 4, 1972

"In coming to contact and recording with those who are of other elements, those who are of other kingdoms, you may do so through the I Am consciousness or the spiritual aspect of yourself rather than through the soul substance, which may have within it certain blockages, memories and patterns that are not suitable to that kind of relationship. . . .

"For this is also the goal of mankind: to have within his experience an interrelationship, a higher form of exchange, with everything that exists; so that everything serves the One, and the One which is in all things is being served and sustained and rewarded.

You thus are fulfilling that which you have come to do, which is to be as a child of God.

"Since God or Spirit exchanges within Itself all Its forms and all the lesser kingdoms without prejudice, then does it not behoove the sons of God, which are the imitators or cocreators with God in His aspect of trinity, to have a similar type of relationship with all form, with all matter, with all Creative Principle?"

– Archangel Uriel; August 18, 1970

Since the beginning of time, mystics, prophets, philosophers and teachers have used the animal kingdom to relate in parable form the certain qualities within man that relate to that kind of thinking, feeling, desire and thought pattern. Since all originated from the one Source, Creative Energy, the patterns that are in each species and in the kinds of animals within each species give a universal form or pattern that can be used as a tool to teach the nature of man in the physical dimension.

Jesus taught, "As you do it unto the least of these, you do it unto me."

Gautama Buddha taught, "One thing only do I teach: suffering and the ceasing of suffering. Kindness to all living creatures is the true religion."

Mohammed said to his followers, "There is no beast on Earth, nor bird which flies with its wings, but the same is of people like unto you."

The entire philosophy of Albert Schweitzer affirms that love must transcend man's narrow ethical systems at present, and that love of and reverence for all life must become the pivotal concept of our behavior in the Aquarian Age.

KARMA

Since humanity shares this planet with other living forms, we are to learn our lessons from living with them on this home, school, dimension. Our acts, our thoughts, our feelings, good and bad, result in good and bad reactions in the same proportion. This is balance, harmony, cause and effect, or karma.

Dr. Gina Cerminara in her book *Many Lives, Many Loves,* writes:

"I recall in the Edgar Cayce files wherein a person reaped good or bad karma with regard to the animal kingdom; but the principle would undoubtedly hold true with this as with any other sphere of nature. On the strength of the whole drift of the Cayce material, then, I believe this proposition can be fairly stated:

"A man's attitude toward and treatment of animals is karma-producing, and the karmic reaction good or bad comes to him from the animal kingdom itself. This is merely a more formalized and specific way of saying: What you do comes back to you. . . . Cast your bread upon the water and you shall find it, after many days."

In a soul intunement which I gave on October 4, 1972, to a very advanced light worker who was having an extremely difficult time in overcoming a serious bodily dysfunction, it was revealed: "In Atlantis you were a research laboratory scientist experimenting with animals. You understood and accepted the concept of the common elements making up and comprising the physical vehicle of all forms, both animal and man. Therefore, your comprehension made you more responsible than someone who was ignorant of this understanding. You were rather cold and impersonal. You were unfeeling and lacked emotional rapport in your relationships.

"Therefore, when you played with hormones and chemicals, to change and to reorganize the physical vessel in which these animals were living–and you did accept that they also had consciousness separate and above that physical vessel–it did not disturb you that you altered them and their form to the extent that you did. Some of the things you did were quite grotesque, not for the sake of deformity but for the sake of scientific curiosity.

"For instance, you would overfeed farm and food-supplying animals to see how large you could make them in order to get more food from each one. Money or commerce probably was part of the motive. Your strongest motives, however, were research and power.

"So, by forcing growth and evolutionary patterns you actually tortured those animals, who were prisoners to you since they had no way of opposing you. Now you are paying that karma emotionally, mentally and physically by going through the same process that you have put others through, even though those others were of a lesser intelligence and could not communicate this to you at the time.

"The law of cause and effect, through the elements which we all commonly share on this planet, works through your body as those elements worked through the bodies of those you experimented with without feeling. Forgiveness of yourself and your past actions is now the major key."

LOVE

The higher law of *Love God and Love One Another* balances out all error conditions and the law of karma. Light workers, just as the one in the soul intunement mentioned above, have the responsibility during these Latter Days to forgive consciously the past errors of themselves and of the entire race of man in relationship to the abuses they have perpetrated against the animal kingdoms and all the other kingdoms upon the planet Earth.

"That you are light workers means that you work *with* the light or *in* the light or *for* the light of that consciousness which is Spirit. Therefore, you must at all times adhere to the highest principles and to the most conscientious analysis when you think of disturbing those elements and those forms in whatever way they are expressing. Provided they are not destroying or undermining your evolvement and development, they have the right and the freedom to express, and must have that proper respect and opportunity; with your guidance, with your supervision and with your guardianship, in fulfilling the roles you have as sons of man evolving into sons of God or the Light Itself. . . .

"The light workers must develop this conscientious attitude and must work together as a unified whole. When you are dealing with an entire kingdom, such as the realms of animal, vegetable or mineral life form as you now know them expressing upon the Earth, you as an individual light worker are not strong enough, nor is it your responsibility nor can it be your function, to determine an entire breed, kingdom or evolutionary species. It must be with the concerted action, the concerted agreement of the one hundred and forty-four thousand light workers, minimum. For this is representative and symbolic as well as powerfully indicative on the so-called material or manifesting realm of action.

"Therefore, when the light workers are embodied in the form of spiritual consciousness on the Earth and are connected or coordi-

nated specifically in that number and for a divine, unified purpose, they as one voice and in one agreement can control, can conduct and can guide the species which we have enumerated here."
– Sananda; April 4, 1972

"As you [the light workers] achieve power over the elements in your body, so you will achieve and will balance those in the other forms of Earth and will bring Earth back into its proper, total state of purity–the state of Eden, so-called–in which all are in proper form, all are in proper relationship, all are in proper harmony with one another; and the form of man, as a child of God, can have power over, and work with, all in love, peace and justice. That divine love, which I spoke of in the beginning, for all life form and energy will be achieved and will be exercised and will be executed by the Sonship, through God, of man by the year 2000. Amen."
– Archangel Uriel; July 29, 1970

As Nada, my I Am Self aspect, stated on February 4, 1970: "My single feature for this is bringing about a total love responsibility unto all life form, whether it be in the race structure of man as a being or in the lower forms of life or in the higher forms of creation that can be of assistance to the race of man. Unless we can be humble before those who are higher in structure and evolvement, and strong for those who are lesser in understanding and evolvement, then we cannot portray the fourth dimensional frequency development that is ours to behold and to be taken seriously with this love responsibility of which I now speak and inform you. So be it!"

HARMONY OF MIND

by El Morya/Mark
Cofounder, with Nada-Yolanda, of Mark-Age, Inc.

MALE AND FEMALE

So God created man in His image, in the image of God created He him; male and female created He them. — Genesis 1:27

Although this statement concerning our nature and makeup reveals more than one significant truth, we are considering here only that which has to do with our phases of mind and their proper relationship within our individual being. Thus, although this scripture has profound meaning to our spiritual, mental and physical being, we shall examine the mental here. This will reveal the divine harmony of our mind and will give divine authority for the proper exercise of control by each individual.

Each of the seven scriptural quotations discussed will disclose immediately its full significance when just several word substitutions are made.

For *male, man* and *husband,* substitute *conscious mind* or *will.*

For *female, woman* and *wife,* substitute *subconscious mind* or *soul.*

As we will see when examining I Corinthians 11:3, this gives us the finite relationship, represented by the two aspects of infinite Trinity: the Father and the Holy Spirit, or Divine Mind and divine law. Our counterpart, made in God's likeness, is our will and our soul.

The message thus stands out in amazing simplicity and clarity. The function of the conscious mind, or will, is to speak the word, while that of the subconscious mind is to see to the fulfilling of that word, as well as to maintaining contact with Divine Mind, as a two-way channel between God and man; also, to maintain the body in perfect working condition. This has been well known. But the divine

125

EL MORYA/MARK
1922–1981
Metaphysical interpretation of the
Bible was central to Mark's teaching

plan and authority for its proof in the scriptures has not been noted or stressed sufficiently.

While it has been known that any variation from this pattern of harmony results in varying degrees of mental disharmony, the proper spiritual treatment, as given by the Holy Bible, has not been recognized. A study of these treatments as given by Jesus, Paul and Peter will enable one to "cast out demons" properly, thus restoring the true mental balance and harmony.

Let us see what light is revealed when these substitutions, plus several others, are made in the following passages. The remaining quotations are taken from the interlinear translations of the original Greek of the Vatican manuscript #1209, as found in the Emphatic Diaglott.

Mark 10:6–9: *But from the beginning of creation a male and a female He made them. "On account of this shall a man leave his father and mother. And the two shall be into one flesh." So that no longer are they two, but one flesh. Then what God has joined together, man disunites not.* – Jesus

The male and female principles inherent in one individual, either man or woman, as disclosed by both of the preceding quotations, are more clearly understood if we realize that *them* in these passages refers to many such individuals, as both male and female polarities or aspects in one person; not meaning many persons, with some as male and some as female. Perhaps this would be clearer if you substituted *him,* referring to generic man, for *them.*

There is one significant point revealed by the first line of this passage, but as it is not directly related to this chapter, it just will be noted. That is the word *a* instead of *the* in the phrase *"from a begin-*

ning." The Greek definitely does not say *the,* and this is true also in John 1:1.

Therefore, what commonly has been interpreted as a statement referring to the beginning of time is not so meant. Rather, it refers to this particular creation of this plane of human consciousness known as our universe. This long has been known by metaphysicians who realize the story of creation as given in Genesis is not only how God creates on an infinite scale, but also how we create on our finite and worldly scale: "in a beginning" or "in beginning" anything that is to be manifested.

"On account of this shall a man leave his father and mother." For, "in a beginning" (at his birth) a man "shall leave" (as distinguished from an individual, a distinct personality, within Divine Mind) "his father and mother" (his Father-Mother God Creator).

"'And the two shall be into one flesh.' So that no longer are they two, but one flesh." The conscious and the subconscious are united as one mind within the body. They are not two separate minds, but one harmonious mind with different functions in the same body, representing a single personality or man.

"Then what God has joined together, man disunites not." God has given us a sound mind, a peaceful and harmonious mind. Let man know this and not disrupt this harmony by upsetting, or by letting be upset, the natural balance.

This is the function of the will. It should sift all thoughts entering into one's mind, either consciously or subconsciously, by reeducation and by allowing the cleansing action of Holy Spirit to eliminate all thoughts that are already in, or seek to enter, the subconscious; that is, all thoughts that are not from God. Jesus told us this in the parable of the thieves who could not break into the strong man's house (mind, body) until they had bound him (his will).

PROPER INTERPRETATION OF WIFE

Ephesians 5:21–33: . . . *submitting yourselves to each other in fear of Christ: wives to their own husbands as to the Lord; because a husband is head of the wife, even as Christ is head of the congregation; he is preserver of the body. But as the congregation is subjected to Christ, thus also wives to husbands in everything. Husbands, love your wives even as Christ also loved the congregation, and delivered himself up on its behalf, so that he might sanctify it, having cleansed in the bath of water by a word; so that he might place the glorious congregation beside himself, having not a spot or blemish or any such things, but that it might be holy and blameless. Thus are husbands obligated to love their wives, as their own bodies. He who loves his wife, loves himself; for no one ever hated his own flesh, but nourishes and cherishes it, even as Christ the congregation; because we are members of his body. "On account of this shall a man leave his father and mother, and shall be closely joined to his wife, and the two will be into one flesh." This secret is great, but I speak about Christ and about the congregation. But also every one of you, let each one love his wife as himself; and so that the wife may reverence the husband.*

Ephesus symbolizes the building center or faculty of man, and corresponds to that faculty represented by Judas Iscariot, the life conserver.

Note the clause in this scripture: *"he is preserver of the body,"* wherein we are told that we are being instructed, in this epistle, in such body rebuilding and preservation. The recognition and the maintenance of the proper divinely given mental and spiritual harmony are of primary importance to our spiritual regeneration, as well as to our mental and physical preservation.

This scripture is one which has been so grossly misapplied, by being limited in interpretation by man, that untold millions of wives, and subsequently families, have been denied full expression of their God-ordained freedom, having been subjected to various degrees in ways never intended or even implied by Paul.

Yet, Paul sought to avoid this, where he specifically points out: (1) the preceding discussion did not apply to marriages, but rather to a spiritual principle, and (2) although this message was not meant to apply to man-made marriages, nevertheless it is well for both husband and wife to love each other, and for the wife to reverence the husband.

However, no command is given in these two lines to the wife to be in subjection to the husband. So, let us see to what Paul referred when he said: *"This secret is great, but I speak about Christ and about the congregation."*

Before examining this passage for its spiritual message, let us once more look at the clue to the meaning of the entire passage. Paul is speaking here of Christ as the Christ indwelling each of us, the I Am within everyone, not just Christ Jesus as a specific, external personality. *Congregation* refers to a group of thoughts, particularly in this message to religious and spiritual thoughts.

Remember, we are being instructed in the proper harmony of man's mind and the thoughts (congregation) therein (the body); further, that man is a trinity of spirit, intellect and soul, or of Christ, conscious mind (will, *husband*) and subconscious mind (soul, *wife*). These are the Christ, the husband and the wife of whom Paul speaks, with their resulting congregation (thoughts) in the church (body).

Conscious and subconscious phases of the same mind owe to each other those duties and functions ordained to each, and are not to usurp control over functions designated to the other.

For example, the conscious mind is that part of us which should make decisions relative to our actions as a whole, such as what to say, where to go and what to do. In like manner, the subconscious mind has such specific functions as control of the body when asleep, or repairing the body and keeping it in proper working condition, and adjusting the body to varying external and internal factors, such as heat and emotion.

One prime example of such harmonious working according to divinely ordained pattern is the operation of the body. The conscious (will) makes a decision relative to performing a certain act, after which the subconscious (soul) transmits that thought into the proper electrical, chemical and mechanical impulses necessary to have the body perform that action.

It is not the right of the subconscious to question that order or to disobey. And the conscious mind is not able to tell the subconscious how to perform those actions. So, under the silent watch of the inner Christ, each must perform or function as ordained, not attempting to replace the other.

"Wives to their own husbands as to the Lord" will be more clear if you insert *the same* before *as*. Thus, the soul answers to both the Christ and the will, to the spiritual and to the intellectual in man.

Nothing but God's good comes from the Christ Self. But listening to only the intellectual, when it is not spiritually illumined, causes man his troubles.

One of Paul's statements, due to misinterpretation, long has caused unnecessary and improper hardship to wives and to women in general. Paul is telling us something that is vitally important, but not what has been imagined. He really said: *"because the conscious* (will) *is head of* (has authority over) *the subconscious* (soul), *even as the Christ* (spiritual, I Am Self within) *is the head of* (has authority over) *his thoughts; he* (the will) *is preserver of the body."*

PROPER MANIFESTATION

With the Christ level of your mind in charge of your spiritual thoughts, the intellectual level of your mind must employ properly your reasoning powers and your will so as to instruct the subconscious level of your mind in the proper things to be manifested in your body so that it will be preserved as a medium through which your entire being can operate on this plane of existence.

If the conscious impresses negative thoughts of lack of health and of specific or general ailments and body deficiencies, the subconscious automatically sets about to record such impressions (actually commands) as conditions of the body.

But the conscious also can impress only positive thoughts of God's perfection for our bodies, and the subconscious then will record (or will not superimpose upon) God's perfect life throughout our bodies.

A significant directive is embodied in these words of Paul, for the wife's own husband (soul's own conscious mind) is to be the one giving such impressions. We have the conscious power to be the only intellect that gives these impressions to our own subconscious.

We have the right to say that no negative thoughts of anyone else or of the race consciousness may cause our subconscious to record any condition other than health in our bodies. That directive may be given as a standing order to the subconscious mind, not only as concerns negative outside thoughts of health but as concerns all our thoughts not initiated or not accepted by our Christ Selves or our conscious minds. In this capacity we can more fully act as the preserver of the body.

But, as noted before, the intellect is not always dependable. We cannot expect that the subconscious will manifest only in truth if the commands given by the conscious are not in line with the principles of truth.

The subconscious mind, or soul, is the initial link with the Christ mind, but it is also subject to the intellect. So, although the soul may know that a certain thought of the intellect will produce an error condition, its function is not to argue.

However, as intellect recognizes truth and seeks to be guided by it, our souls will receive more and more proper thoughts, and heaven will draw ever nearer. Then we reach the point where we realize we may not always know consciously the proper thoughts to submit or to reject.

Then we can issue a standing directive to our subconscious that it be guided by our indwelling Christ mind, asking that "your will, not mine, be done." Then, as we reach the unfoldment where the Christ mind and the intellectual mind become one, we have accomplished what Paul writes: *"as* [when] *the congregation* [all our thoughts] *is sub-jected to Christ* [spiritual man within]. *"*

When every thought is thus based on truth only, we truly will benefit by the subconscious acting on our conscious thoughts: *"thus also wives to husbands in everything."*

DIVORCE

This is an appropriate time to call attention to, without discussing, biblical references to divorce. You may now see why there should be no separation or *divorce* of the subconscious and the conscious phases of our minds.

This *marriage* was made in heaven, and neither an improperly performing conscious or subconscious should be cast out or disobeyed. For the time will come when, as noted in the scriptures, a husband or a wife (conscious or subconscious) may be the means of the other's salvation. Both Jesus and Moses used this spiritual meaning when referring to divorce, distinguishing between God-made and man-made marriages.

The rest of this passage becomes self-explanatory when the substitutions are made for *husband* and *wife*. Boldly, Paul reveals this message: *"He who loves his wife* [soul or subconscious], *loves himself; for no one ever hated his own flesh."*

It may be well to note here why husband and wife were used to represent the conscious and the subconscious levels of our one mind. Simply put: those terms were not coined as yet, and the idea of two minds was not common. So, in cases where there is as yet no adequate conception of a new idea, and therefore there are no words to convey the meaning of such an idea, symbolism must be used, in terms of something familiar to those hearing the idea. In addition, in that part of the world, parables are the most worthy and enjoyed form of teaching.

COOPERATION

Colossians 3:18–19: *Wives, submit to your husbands, as has been proper in the Lord. Husbands, love your wives, and be not embittered against them.*

Again Paul tells us that the subconscious (wife) is to submit to the conscious (husband). But he gives us a relationship between conscious and subconscious that all students of the mind would do well to contemplate.

It long has been taught that the subconscious is like an animal, as regards intelligence and emotions. We have been told many ways to subdue and to train the subconscious, almost in the same manner we would an animal. The subconscious is supposed to be unreasonable, to refuse to cooperate, to delight in playing tricks on the conscious, to withhold information, to be careless about the welfare of the conscious mind or the body, to refuse to be serious, and so on.

All of this may seem to have some basis in fact, but that is not its nature. The subconscious has many false impressions registered upon it, and many confusing and contradictory ones. It does its best. But some things are impossible, such as fulfilling both the negative and the positive directions of the same request.

What happens when results do not seem to coincide with the supposed request? The subconscious is accused and various degrees of abuse are heaped on it. Does that help matters any? If we recognize the subconscious as possessing of intelligence and as being the seat of the emotions, how can we expect such unfounded attacks on it to have no effect?

Shall we say that the part of the mind which controls the emotions has no feeling? How much closer would the conscious and the subconscious be if the conscious would attempt to search out the cause of failure rather than to pass the blame. How much more would be accomplished if, as Paul advises, the conscious loves the subconscious (soul) and is not embittered against it.

So, let us stop underestimating, insulting and condemning the subconscious in any way. If desired results are not forthcoming, try accepting the responsibility consciously, and with love and kindness seek the aid of the subconscious.

COVERING THE HEAD

I Corinthians 11:3–12: *But I wish you to have knowledge, that Christ is the head of every man; but of woman, the man; but head of Christ, God. Every man praying or prophesying having something upon the head, disgraces his head. But every woman praying or prophesying with the head uncovered disgraces her head; for it is one and the same it having been shaven. For if a woman is not covered, also let her hair be cut off; but if it is a disgrace to a woman for the hair to be cut off or shaven let her be covered. Indeed for a man it is not fitting for the head to be covered, being a likeness and glory of God; but a woman is man's glory; for man is not from woman, but woman from man, for man was not created on account of woman, but woman on account of man. On account of this is it fitting for woman to have authority on the head, on account of messengers. But neither woman without man, nor man without woman, in the Lord. For as woman from man, so also man through woman; but all things out of God.*

This is another message of Paul's that, for lack of spiritual understanding, has been misinterpreted in a preposterous literal manner. Granted that confused translation has helped to foster this, it is going too far afield to declare it a mortal sin for a woman to be in church without a covering on her head.

This is in direct contradiction to what Jesus taught about the outside of man being unimportant, as compared to the inside, or what he thought. Let's not become involved, either, with literalness by saying that a woman is not a man. In the generic sense, there is no distinction whatever regarding the entire personality.

Paul plainly tells us here that the spiritual aspect in man—I Am, Christ—is the highest level of mind in man and has authority (the head) over the entire man. But this spiritual man or Christ mind is not supreme or alone in the universal divine plan. God is.

Within the individual personality, or man, the relative chain of command is first superconscious (Christ), then the conscious (man), and then the subconscious (woman).

The complete relationship is: God (infinite Mind), Christ (I Am Self within each of us), intellect (conscious mind, will) and soul (subconscious mind).

The infinite and finite parallel is: God (infinite knower) and I Am Self (infinite agent), as compared to conscious will (finite intelligence) and soul (finite agent).

As for the meaning where Paul states it is a disgrace for a man to have something upon his head when praying or prophesying, it takes but little word substitution to reveal the proper interpretation.

"Every intellect or will (man) *affirming* (praying) *or decreeing* (prophesying) *that covers or overrules* (has something on) *the Christ mind* (his head), *disgraces his Sonship* (Christ, his head)."* Let an unillumined intellect attempt to override the Christ within, to ignore his divine nature, and he disgraces his spiritual Self, created in God's image and likeness.

In like manner: *"But every subconscious or soul* (woman) *praying or prophesying with the conscious or will* (the head) *having no knowledge of such action* (uncovered, or apart from, out from under the authority of), *disgraces the conscious* (head); *for it is one and the same thing, it having been cut off from the conscious* (shaven)."*

Inasmuch as the subconscious is to submit to the conscious, it may not act on its own volition regarding anything not divinely assigned to it, but must act only on the decrees of the will or of the Christ when it has been advised consciously to do so.

It is well to note here that the Christ level of mind does not interfere until the conscious becomes aware of the Christ presence and seeks its guidance. That is, the Christ does not interfere directly, although it may attempt to counsel the intellect through intuition when it is able to attract attention in this manner.

What is to happen when the subconscious does act on its own in unauthorized manner? This verse reveals the answer: *"let her hair be cut off."* Hair represents vitality, so the soul's vitality or energy to carry out such action is to be cut off.

The next verse reminds us that since the spiritual man is the Christ, the image and the likeness of God, it is not fitting for intellectual man to act other than is spiritually proper.

But the soul is for the proper use of the will. Why is this so? *"For the will or intellect* (man) *is not from the subconscious or soul* (woman), *but subconscious* (woman) *from conscious* (man), *for the conscious* (man) *was not created on account of the subconscious* (woman), *but the subconscious* (woman) *on account of the conscious* (man)*."*

The conscious personality (man) was created in God's Mind as a separate identity, with the right to use consciously as much of God's power as it could comprehend. The subconscious phase of this personality was given to this conscious mind as the link with infinite Mind (divine agent), or actually as conscious man's (will or intellect) use of Divine Mind, thus enabling him to have his thoughts manifested.

A further explanation is given. Since, according to divine plan, this method of the will instructing an obedient subconscious is the proper method of man's ideating and manifesting (*"On account of this is it fitting"*), the subconscious must not act independently. It must act only on the decree of the higher Self (*"for woman to have authority on the head"*), since divine ideas from God come through the higher Self (*"on account of messengers"; messengers* commonly translated as *angels,* representing divine ideas or agents in the Christ consciousness).

But neither the subconscious nor the conscious is to act independently in man. For just as the subconscious acts on instructions from the conscious will (*"For as woman from man"*), so also the wishes of the will are performed through the subconscious (*"so also man through woman"*). *"But all things out of God":* all ideas that are of reality (truth) are by and from Divine Mind.

SUBMISSION OF SUBCONSCIOUS

I Timothy 2:11–12: *In quietness let a woman learn, with all submission. But I do not permit a woman to teach, nor to assume authority over man, but to be in silence.*

This passage needs no further explanation, once the substitution of *subconscious* for *woman* and of *conscious* for *man* has been made.

However, this verse gives us a perfect spiritual treatment, with scriptural authority, for effecting mental cures where the subconscious has gained dominion over the conscious. Speak these words to such a person, being yourself fully aware that this is a prescribed treatment and one which the domineering subconscious must recognize as of divine origin.

I Peter 3:1–7: *In like manner wives, submitting yourselves to your own husbands, so that if some are disobedient to the word, through their wives' conduct they may be gained without a word, having seen in fear your pure conduct. . . . Husbands in like manner, according to knowledge dwelling with the female as with a weaker vessel, bestowing honors as also being joint heirs of the gracious gift of life, in order that your prayers may not be hindered.*

When the unillumined intellect thinks in an erroneous manner, thus setting in motion error causes that can manifest only in error conditions, the subconscious should not disregard those instructions but should proceed to manifest those error conditions, exactly in accordance with divine law.

Then, when our intellect that is not thinking according to truth (*"are disobedient to the word"*) sees that the manifested effects of our thoughts are not what we wanted (*"through their wives' conduct"*: the manifested condition being the conduct of the subconscious), our intellect by itself may come to understand that such conditions are the result of our own wrong thinking, and may seek the way of truth (*"they may be gained without a word"*).

Such an intellect may seek self-improvement through fear that continued wrong action may result in more failures manifesting (*"having seen in fear your pure conduct"*: according to divine law of cause and effect).

Peter cautions us even more clearly than does Paul in Colossians 3:19, regarding loving our subconscious and not being embittered against it. This message of Peter's is so startlingly clear that it cannot be improved upon. It is a perfect plan for the ideal marriage of aspects of our individual minds.

When this plan is followed there need be no fear of subconscious blocks that prevent full cooperation between the conscious and subconscious levels of our one mind. Then the subconscious, which is our link with infinite Mind, will not block our prayers, affirmations, decrees and realizations from rising to Divine Consciousness.

Instead it will do all it can, which is far more than nearly every one of us has yet realized, to aid us in our spiritual unfoldment as well as in our outer world. Remember, your soul is a two-way channel between God and you. Cultivate its cooperation in love, and your progress will be astonishing and fruitful.

&

Note by Yolanda: These concepts of Christ or superconscious, conscious and subconscious aspects of the one mind of man are limited concepts designed for the metaphysical interpretations of biblical scriptures. As such they are presented for basic understanding of what have been gross misinterpretations of such scriptures.

For greater spiritual understanding of these concepts of aspects of one mind, please see the Mark-Age books *How To Do All Things, MAPP* to Aquarius: *Mark Age Period & Program, Evolution of Man, Angels and Man,* and numerous other Mark-Age booklets and tapes.

SPIRITUAL
UNDERSTANDING OF SEX

CONQUEST OF THE FLESH

(Regarding continence and self-conquest of the flesh.) "In order to arrive at the spiritual perfection which you desire, it is necessary to make this conquest. For the sexual drive is only placed in the animal part of man and the creatures of Earth for the purpose of reproduction. But man has elaborated and has emphasized it to the point where it is the single motivating factor in his life. This is especially true in your American country. It had been true in many similar cultures throughout history and was the main reason for their eventual downfall.

"This is not too easy to accept. But underlying the falsity, the pretense, the false values of civilizations in this drive to satisfy the sexual urge is the root of all physical desires and greed, among them the drive for pleasure in eating, in luxuries for the body, the ease and comfort without the necessary enjoyment of using one's native intelligence and talents to bring about such comforts and luxuries. Out of this comes the drive for power, the power which is the anti-Christ. It is as simple as that. Power as organized by man is the force which denies and protests against God Himself. For God is the only power in the universe. God power is the power through which all things are made manifest. . . .

"Man is God's creation, not God man's. Whenever man realizes this and gives to God His rightful role and returns to God the power which is God's and which God has given in His graciousness to His sons, then there can be the true peace, the true salvation, the true union with God which all men yearn for in their experiences here on Earth and later in spirit. None escapes from the soul-yearning for the oneness with this beginning. The beginning and the end are the

139

Father. All men yearn to be in the beginning and to know the end. Therefore, they yearn for the One who can give them this oneness, beginning and end. Sooner or later man must return to this. He then will be pure and whole and truly returned to his rightful role: Sonship with God, lord of the universe."

— Paul the Apostle; March 25, 1958

TRUE UNION

"You cannot aid your brother by furthering his false illusions. The pleasure in the union of sex is like a drug which covers up the channel from receiving higher inspiration, thoughts and divine guidance. This may be difficult to accept, but we wish you to do your best in listening to the inner voice which guides you always. It tells you what we tell you: sex is substitute for union with God. In sex, man is trying to unite with God, because God is in each one of his sisters and brothers.

"No matter how man manifests the sex act he is truly seeking union with God. He may force another and conquer the other person's appetite, but even here he is manifesting his inner desire to force himself on God, to conquer God and to be supreme over the Father. This of course is impossible, as many acts and thoughts of men are impossible, but nevertheless that is what man is trying to do. In his animal passions he is seeking a lower expression of a higher desire.

"You cannot contribute to this delusion if you truly wish to aid your fellowman, because you then are allowing mortal desires to supersede immortal desires. You are letting your lower self conquer higher purpose. We know you desire to give aid to your fellowmen, but sometimes aid is not aid he or she thinks is aid. Sometimes the opposite of what another person desires is the true, Godly aid. When one prays to the Father for a specific gift, the Father often realizes that fulfilling that specific desire would deter and harm His beloved child. So, He answers with an opposite gift or a withholding of the gift. . . . The Father is the judge of all that is good.

"By giving your brother sexual satisfaction you may delay him from his rightful discovery that sex is a substitute for what he truly has been seeking from you and from all life here on Earth. By granting sympathy to your sister you are deterring her from the realization that she has not right to sympathy or self-pity, but must face the consequences of her wrong thoughts and actions of years and lifetimes past. Give only the God love and light within you and you give all."

— John the Divine; May 4, 1958

RELATIONSHIPS WITH OTHERS

"You are free to choose your companions at all times. We do not insist on certain unions, whether there is basic karmic association or not. That choice is always yours to make and it is yours to break. But if you do undertake a certain union and then forfeit the obligation of fulfilling that which you have taken upon yourselves, you create a karmic debt which somehow, somewhere, sometime must be paid. . . .

"We state a fundamental law which operates in all spheres of all realms of God's kingdom. . . . When two souls have intertwined their karmic debts it becomes purposeful and expedient to fulfill them individually and combined. In this too is God's symbolic reference. For we fulfill ourselves as individual souls, we fulfill the race of mankind jointly, and furthermore we fulfill and regenerate the power of God. This is the truth in all unions and is given as an example in a specific case and in the case of all groups who are used collectively, whether the groups consist of two or more millions, such as in the case of nations, or the races of mankind."

— Paul the Apostle; April 1, 1958

ENERGY EXCHANGE

"It is extremely important that we begin to understand the inflow and the outflow of energies. Energy is Spirit. Spirit is Energy. Each man, each creation in the animal, vegetable, mineral kingdoms of the Earth plane is Spirit or Energy. Each is vibrating at his own individual rate. Not only is the individual manifestation operating within a certain frequency but each unit of that creation has a particular vibration of its own within that frequency limit. No two things in creation are exactly alike. Thereby does the Father know each sparrow, each raindrop, each man is His own product. . . .

"Cosmic or Christ consciousness is a vibrational rate you will be stepping into. That rate is already established. You individually are orbiting or in motion at a rate different from that of the Christ rate of vibration, and shall be stepping into it.

"Spirit, sensing Its own needs, attracts or repels, as the case may be, those other spiritual manifestations, be they places or persons, which can aid in the operation of this change. Therefore, those in your orbit are necessary to you at the given moment they are there. Each and every incident, each and every exchange of thought, of word and of deed has its place in your development. It should be with a sense of continuous thanksgiving that every single thought, word and event is occurring to the individual, not only the individual person but the individual object and the individual planet upon which you are placed.

"All is a matter of service. None are higher and none are lower. All is Spirit vibrating at a different frequency. Therefore, it should be considered service to be in the thought or the physical relationship of any and of all with whom there is any connection. It is an exchange of service, Spirit serving Spirit; for there is nothing but Spirit. There is never anything out of its proper place. However, as cocreators you can always change or raise that situation or consciousness by expecting and asking for the spiritual counterpart, the service of Spirit, to do this.

"How does Spirit serve Itself? By exchange. By setting up a bank of withdrawals and deposits. Let us look at the elements; or nature, as you think of it. In the animal kingdom, in the vegetable kingdom and in the mineral kingdom it is an exchange of giving and taking, receiving and spending, a breathing in and a breathing out. There is nothing which when dedicated to Spirit cannot be exchanged.

"Dedicated to self it is a depletion of the bank on the part of the person who is involved, regardless of whether he or she thinks he is receiving or taking. I repeat: if it is dedication or satisfaction or gratification of self it depletes the one who is in any way involved, even unconsciously involved. If it is dedication with the understanding of Spirit and what Spirit is, a mass of Energy operating at a certain frequency and vibrational rate, there is nothing that cannot be exchanged in order to raise or to make a better balance within the manifestation being served. . . .

"Energy is Spirit. Spirit is Energy. Spirit manifesting on many levels, Energy expressing in various frequency vibrations, feeding and renewing Itself, dispensing and refurnishing Itself. This is the function of Spirit. In the natural world of the three-dimensional plane, energy is met and renewed on all three levels it represents. When energy in a plant is spent in one direction on the physical, it will receive energies on that same level or physical frequency, though from another element. This is complementary and necessary.

"So it is in mental and in the spiritual worlds. You cannot spend Energy or Spirit manifesting at a certain vibrational rate in one way, such as physical, and refurnished or renewed at another frequency vibration, such as on the mental, and expect results that are proper to keep the balance. So it is with man and so it is with a planet. As the energies of the cosmos, these divine love vibrations are projected into the Earth's atmosphere and recorded and received by the men and women living on that planet. So it must be expressed in kind or in the same vibrational rate.

"That is why it is so necessary now for the planet and the people on it to receive, through the mass educational program, the information that those who are key lights have to offer. It is true that the energies that are coming into the planet now are coming from a higher or a fourth dimensional etheric plane; or are spiritual energies. Therefore, man has to be educated as to how he can spend those spiritual energies that are already in him and are building up in him a greater bank account. This will be done through educating him as to his true spiritual and divine nature: a cocreator with spiritual Energy, a son of God, a worker of miracles.

"It is thought by many who are in the spiritual work or are very highly evolved spiritually or who have developed very high morality rates because of their spiritual studies that God is not interested in the material world. Yet we tell you this truth: God manifests, or Spirit or Energy is manifested, on every level of expression. There is no difference to Spirit or Energy in the etheric manifestation, the mental manifestation or the physical manifestation. All are different rates of vibration. Therefore, the spending and receiving, the giving and taking, the expending and renewing of energies on the physical are as important as they are on the mental and spiritual. For all is Spirit, all is one, all is being returned unto All.

"If man can but realize that his physical manifestation is but an energy frequency vibration and nothing more, then he would not set up laws, ideas and wrong conceptions about how he exchanges his physical energies one with the other. The same applies to the mental world and to the spiritual. Of course, in the spiritual world all has become purified and there are not the misconceptions any longer. But in the physical and in the mental realms still remain many of the misconceptions, still is the lack of the refinement and of spiritual or Godlike qualities.

"But it is our intention to raise or to change the rates of vibration that now exist in the physical world and in the mental realms to that of a spiritual understanding, to understand that all is energy vibrating as its own natural frequency. When this is understood, then purity is possible in every realm of expression. This must be made manifest on the Earth planet before the coming of the entire mass Christ consciousness permits the return of the Master or the Prince of Peace. So, it is part of your training and understanding to realize and to work with the physical as much as it is to work with the mental and the spiritual.

"Each of the realms with which the Earth plane is involved—mental, physical and spiritual—has an octave or a range of experiences or expressions. In the physical you have the five senses. In the mental you have imagination and thought control. In the spiritual you have feeling and divine love. The spiritual encompasses all that is in the mental and the physical. The mental encompasses all that is on the physical. The physical is limited to the physical five senses, but it is in no way less a spiritual or a God manifestation than the world of spiritual expression.

"Where man has erred in his concepts has been where he has expressed any of these experiences for the sake of the experience itself and not for the sake of the spiritual enlightenment and evolution, the return of Spirit to Spirit, the growth of energy, the expansion of consciousness. Therefore, when you find on the physical, mental or even in the spiritual that it is for the sake of the experience itself and not for the sake of spiritual exchange, then you are in

144

danger of self-gratification, self-glory and self-expression. This of course is meant for the lower self; not for the higher Self which is God Self, Spirit, and is to be expressed for that purpose.

"We come now to that very paradoxical and controversial subject that on the Earth has resulted in many misconceptions, that of sexual energy. In our concept and in the higher concepts the meaning of sexual energy is life force or spiritual God Force in action. Therefore, there is sexual exchange on the spiritual realm as in the mental realm as in the physical realm. But again we speak in terms of lower self and higher Self. If at any time there is an exchange for the gratification or the expression of the lower self, this is the danger point.

"If the exchange of life force on the spiritual, mental or physical levels is for the exchange of spiritual energies or for high Self expression or for the payment and the deposit of energies, we find it is for the enhancement of the individual expression in whatever realm it is expressing itself. For these are but means that Spirit has of depositing and withdrawing Its own complementary force fields.

"The so-called sexual exchange is a creative act on any realm; which is quite obvious on the physical realm, not so obvious on the mental realm and more illusive on the spiritual realm when viewing it with the consciousness of the Earthman's conception. On the mental realm it is the positive and negative thought-balancing to create a thought form that is perfect; neither too much of the negative nor too much of the positive, but always individual, according to the two that are exchanging the thought. This applies to an individual working on a creative project alone or to more than one individual working out a new pattern together. The balance, the harmony must be set up in the thought or mental imagination realm.

"On the spiritual realm it is that sense of divine love feeling and the divine love action, perfectly balanced, perfectly harmonious, that creates a higher form or a higher ideal, a new dimension into which man or any of God's creation can step. This of course is the purpose of the physical exchange: to bring forth higher form, greater evolution in the physical concept of the life on the planet.

"In the time to come when we step into the Golden Era and man and woman on Earth can spend and receive all three levels simultaneously and with the same purpose, you will have the intunement of

Christ-conscious awareness in alignment not only with each to himself but each to one another. Then will the planet know real peace, real harmony, perfect love for the Divine, perfect love for the Energy which is Spirit and Spirit which is energy. Thereby the second commandment can be fulfilled, the commandment of *love ye one another,* for ye are then loving Spirit in the self and in each other manifestation of Spirit. This is truly Christ consciousness. Then is the true exchange, the true realization, the free flow in and out, spending and receiving, giving and taking, Spirit in action, love in action."

—John Mark (author of Gospel of Mark); January 16-17, 1961

INDIVIDUALIZATIONS OF CREATIVE ENERGY

QUESTION: Is there a new teaching, a new understanding on marriage and relationships between men and women for this New Age of Aquarius?

ANSWER: "Absolutely. There is, in this realm as in all realms, and it stems from one principle. All things will stem from one principle: I am Spirit, you are Spirit, all is Spirit; Spirit is Energy, Creative Energy, in action. You will exchange with this Energy as it is best suitable, complementary and supplementary to your own individual fulfillment. This is a general answer to a very specific question. In the realm in which you are speaking, which goes into what you call intimate relations, into the close personal love relations of men and women on the Earth, you will have to learn that all is Spirit, that love you feel on the personal is but a hint of love in the divine.

"In the divine or in the Christ-conscious awareness we see one another as individualizations of spiritual energies. Some are more satisfactory to our vibrations and more helpful to our vibrations than others. It is to those we gravitate and with those we must make our exchanges. But your understanding of personal love and personal intimate contact must also be transmuted, as every other department of your lives must be.

"Furthermore, when it comes to teaching or helping those who seek us out on these questions, my only answer is what I have been told by the Master Jesus himself: sufficient unto the day the problems thereof. As each day presents its problems and its questions and as each day presents the new factors and factions in the problems, you will meet individually and as a group those who have come to help in this transmutation. Sufficient unto their needs, you will have the answers presented to you from the Spirit within. Let the answer flow from Spirit through you. For then when you are teaching you are intuned with that inner, spiritual Self."

—John Mark; May 17, 1961

CELIBACY

QUESTION: I know there are true celibates on Earth today. How is it possible to recognize this in one's self if such is the case? Is it a natural pattern of evolvement, at which all eventually will arrive?

ANSWER: "This is such a delicate question and one that has many ramifications. There is only one answer to this. It is the answer we give on so many things. I think most will understand what I say here. You must go within and find your own answer.

"There are some of you incarnated on the Earth plane today who come from such a high etheric vibration or planet that the practices expressed in the sexual or re-creative, regenerative way on Earth, what is presently evolving on the Earth plane in the three-dimensional way of procreation, are so alien to what you recognize that you cannot function in a similar way to what they do here. You have not been in that vibration recently; nor do you care to participate in the vibration, though you have come to do a work.

"This does touch many thousands of you on the Earth planet right now. It does not mean the entire Earth planet shall be converted very quickly to your state of consciousness, but as we go into the fourth dimension completely it will be taught. Eventually that will be one of the functions that will atrophy on the Earth, or three-dimensional way of expressing; one of the means, one of the various expressions you will lose eventually on your planet, as you will lose many other things.

"This is a very important question. It is a beautiful and important thing for many of you to understand. There is no fear or shame in our realm, nor should there ever be in your thinking. Go within and use not these things for excuses. Go within and find out if it is true spiritual expression."

– St. Germain; May 31, 1961

SOUL MATES AND TWIN SOULS

"As you develop in your soul in order to become absolutely purified in your Christ consciousness, you have many incarnations and many experiences on many realms. Therefore, you have many relationships. From those relationships you have affinities and various component parts or complementary relationships that you recognize wherever you incarnate again, whether it be on the Earth plane or any other plane.

"So, sometimes you meet on the Earth plane, in an incarnation that you are having now, someone with whom you are so familiar and in complete rapport and vibration almost one hundred percent, as you would like to see it. This is a soul mate. But you have soul mates in other places as well. There are many soul mates, if you would allow yourselves, or if Spirit has the desire so to express Itself in that way through you, to have many experiences of soul mating in one incarnation. This does happen very frequently.

"Now we come to a very complicated teaching that you call twin souls. This is one that has caused much heartache and much controversy in many quarters of mystery schools, occult teachings, and even in your more purified metaphysical schools of thought. Twin souls are two polarities. One soul, as it becomes more and more highly evolved, gravitates to one end of the pole or the other. You have incarnations throughout all your experiences as male and female alternatingly; not precisely alternatingly, please do not misunderstand, but you have to experience both ends of the pole at one time or another. There is no rhythm or pattern to these things.

"But as you become more highly evolved and you become closer to the purity of the Christ spirit, you begin to gravitate closer and closer to one end of the pole. In other words, you might take on more male aspects than you do female aspects. At the same time, there is a complementary force being evolved in this particular universe of exactly the opposite. Let us take a man. He evolves, having male and female incarnations, until he gets to the point where he predominantly incarnates as male, because this is going to be the highest expression while he is in the Christ spheres. When he is in the Christ sphere he may be there for millions or billions of years, as you would record time. He gets closer and closer to a Christ personality.

"Take Christ Jesus as an example. As Jesus evolves as a male aspect more and more, there must be the opposite pole incarnating and developing those complementary forces elsewhere in the universe, developing all those female aspects that will balance and will not throw off the whole function of God or spiritual Creative Energy into one side or the other. God is complete balance at all times. So, as this spiritual Energy or Creative Energy force field, which each one is, develops a male aspect, Spirit naturally, normally and automatically develops a female group of aspects to complement and to hold that polarity in its place. This you call twin souls."

— St Germain; May 31, 1961

(*Editor's note.* She who was Mary, mother of Jesus of Nazareth, is the twin soul of Sananda, he who was Jesus in his last incarnation.)

CAUSE AND EFFECT

QUESTION: Will you please clarify the biblical statements regarding husband and wife, man and woman, in their treatment of one another?

ANSWER: "This is well known to those who study spiritually. Man is the active or positive force and the female is the negative or receiving. The two must be joined fully and equally, as it is in Spirit or Creative Energy, to perform a function that is the son or the child.

"Everywhere in the Bible or in other holy scriptures where you have the use of man or wife, or the love aspect of man for woman in different degrees such as you have in your Old Testament—working, in some cases; Jacob working for Leah—you must interpret it as the positive force working its way into balance with the negative force of that particular aspect or that level of consciousness within your own self.

"I would that I could create a desire in all to look thus upon marriage, courtship and love of the sexes in this way: positive action and negative reaction; cause and effect. Know ye not that no two forces or individualizations, with all the forces and backgrounds of those force fields, can come together and not enact the law of cause and effect? Know ye not that it is as important to you, a woman, to have the cause effected in you as it is in the man to have the reaction within himself?

"Know ye not that ye act out these roles with one another for better or for worse until death do ye part? What is death but the end of that cycle? This is the meaning of your marriage on Earth. This is the marriage that exists in heaven; as you call heaven, the other realms beyond the Earth dimension. Every man and woman united must be aware of the cause in themselves and the reaction of that cause, whether it be in the smallest way or in the greatest way, whether it be over the decision to have a child, to buy a home, to take a trip, to create an act of love.

"*Cause and effect.* Cause and effect within each individual which is the man, cause and effect in the individual which is the woman. Cause and effect in the union; which is a force field in itself, a group force field of two. 'Where two or more are gathered, there I Am.' Who is the I Am but your Christ Self within, and the Christ forces which work in and around every two that are gathered? When a child is created of such union, you have the responsibility of cause and effect within another being.

"Know ye not what takes place in life? You have it around in the animal life, in the vegetable kingdom. Have ye not observed for thousands of years upon the Earth planet that ye are still in ignorance and darkness? We cannot accept this in the Christ consciousness any longer, for we know it is not true. We know—the Christ within me and the Christ within you, the one Self, the one living God—that ye are not in ignorance but ye have shut the door in the face of God and will not listen. This is your [mortal] will, not ours.

"Open this door now. You have before you in this question and in this answer the greatest lesson and the most important faculty aspect of Earth civilization. Some of you put a word into the ethers and say it is sex. But it is life force that we are talking about. Action-reaction, male-female, positive-negative. Stop and examine this question and this answer. Know that you need not go any further in meditation than to work in and through and around this relationship with man and woman. For each of us has been born of woman through the cause of man."

— Nada; October 4, 1961

SPIRITUAL ATTAINMENT

"Sexual prowess . . . is not the means by which one can prove his conquest over the light force, for this is not the purpose of the sexual organs or the act of procreation for which these things were created on the physical. They are means to an end on the physical and add nothing to the spiritual stature or to the spiritual understanding. Yet, no one of a spiritual nature will condemn or will look down upon the act of husband and wife in sexual intercourse, because this is the purpose of procreating the race as long as it remains in a third dimensional physical body.

"But by the time you reach a physical expression of an entirely different nature, which is upon astral and etheric planes, you no longer use the same means of procreating the race or of enhancing the spiritual vibratory rate of yourself, of your partner and of the new energies or souls who are introduced into that area of expression."

QUESTION: Does the use of the sexual function in any manner help prepare one for Christ consciousness?

ANSWER: "There is absolutely no precedent for this upon the Earth, at any time, that ever has been successful. In all the patterns I have given for man to follow [in my multiple incarnations throughout the history of the Earth], never once did I imply or give this as the means by which anyone could reach cosmic consciousness or Christ attainment. Christ attainment is a spiritual expression. The sexual use of the energies and the patterns used are strictly physical and will gain only physical adeptness. Nothing spiritual can ever be attained through physical means."

— Sananda; May 17, 1972

SPIRITUAL AWAKENING
OF YOUTH

The promise and the future of the Earth as a spiritual planet lie in the mass awakening of today's youth. What have you come to do? How can you find your soul's purpose and mission? There is a master plan for Earth and you have a part in it. You have been trained for eons of time to bring forth this program, on other planes and planets as well as on Earth in past lives. The veil of ignorance and negativity around the Earth is being lifted in stages, with brotherly love replacing it. Youth's concern for truth is making the difference.

Brotherly love in action is the mode of operation for the Aquarian Age. This intuitive awareness already is prevalent within today's youth. They are demonstrating it in all fields of interest and are crying out for a positive approach in every area of man's endeavors. Instinctively they know love begets love, good begets good, peace begets peace and security for all who share equally this planet and this solar system.

We in our solar system are in a very special period of time, the cleansing and harvest period, and have reached a spiritual crisis involving the Earth and all upon it. It is through the awareness that the crisis is a spiritual one that we gain our present insight and understanding of world events and problems.

Consciously or unconsciously our youth are instruments for cleaning up the errors and for harvesting what is good, practical and functional from our Earth's past history, which is the program of this Mark Age (1960–2000), the forty years of preparation before the onset of the Aquarian Age. Many of those incarnated here now are not familiar with this Earth vibration, in that many have not lived in or are not familiar with this three-dimensional frequency.

153

This strange, new vibration will cause a reaction in many which can express in one of two extremes: an inability to adjust, or an extreme will to fulfill God's plan and purpose. Therefore, you will see young people performing deeds they never have been able to perform on Earth before, and not conforming to behavior patterns as set up by past generations. Many have ingrained perceptions allowing them to see through crystallized trends, and to break them down and to re-form them for higher, better, more simple purposes. Much of the logic and plans of the past no longer can suffice. Old, third dimensional or material modes of life must be transmuted to make way for the new, fourth dimensional or spiritual patterns.

TURN OFF DRUGS, TURN TO GOD

However, it appears some are undecided, or rather unconvinced, as to the values of opposition to the use of drugs as an aid to one's spiritual search. We shall not try to dissuade anyone by means of trite clichés which all no doubt are familiar with, but rather shall bring forth a few aspects of concepts that may have been overlooked and therefore bear consideration.

Sananda channeling through me stated that those who produce an expansion of consciousness via drugs or any forced psychic unfoldment are not to be examples for others, since they cannot teach and cannot demonstrate that expansion at will. It was artificially achieved by chemical means. It therefore is not meaningful spiritually, as it was not self-achieved through communication with one's higher Self.

St. Germain channeling through me put it well when he said that if we try to get free of the Earth through artificial means, ironically we are defeating our own plan; for we are weakening, actually destroying, our grounding in this plane. Without this it is well nigh impossible to attain the magnificent heights to which we aspire, and also to be able to return freely. If we totally cut our grounding we literally have voided any chance for advancement in this incarnation; for we are not of this plane or any other, but must go back and begin again.

In a communication at a Mark-Age youth meeting, Glo-Ria (previously Gloria Lee, 1926–1962, of Cosmon Research Foundation) summed it up for all: "Much has been said on the Earth plane about the system of drugs and how men and women are being affected by the problem. Expressly I wish to mention that they must learn this is unnecessary for the development of their spiritual work which they have come to perform. The God knowledge that is being bestowed upon these who are in difficulties is very detailed and is to be increased in this segment of time you will experience this season.

"No more will it be proper to say the using of drugs is proper. Spirit has declared it is not of use for the overall totality. It serves to take the soul further away in the long run. Some have taken this route and have experienced an enlightenment and a situation in which they have learned a great deal. This is good, in its aspect. But many have not the strength and the stability to get back onto the pathway after they have been affected in the outer bodies by these drugs. It is an unnecessary tributary to the river of Spirit.

"Those who have taken drugs or are using them now are not to feel that Spirit looks down upon them or is reprimanding them; but is only requesting, in behalf of the Christ Self within these individuals, that they may be awakened to the honesty within and see the truth as it lies securely and awaiting. Notification has been sent . . . on this, for it is a question that has been asked of Spirit by many God-seeking and God-loving individuals—not only in this nation but around this sphere—for clarification and understanding.

"This is what is needed by the youth and young-adult population. They want so much to serve and to give their lives to Spirit that they temporarily try what they inwardly know to be a detour. It is wise to remember we are here to serve Spirit and Spirit's rules. But in the process we must not break man's rules. . . . Do not look upon another as in sin, but see him or her as changed and understanding, and delivered from all evil. For that one is the spirit and the power and the glory. He/she is of God, and you are likewise."

Glo-Ria offered this guidance to one young light worker on August 22, 1969: "You are of God. As a light worker of great potential you have the satisfying responsibility to be the example, the strong one, to demonstrate your cessation of drug usage for your weaker brothers and sisters.

"By your exampling, the true meaning of being a demonstrator of God is discovered and realized. This denial and abstinence gives

155

much-needed strength to the mass subconscious mind, and works on each individual within the race from the inner planes. Each then can find extra added power to resist and to cease the use of such illusionary dead ends and can reach into oneself more easily. Thus, from one's own strengthened will it becomes the individual's own idea to turn off drugs and to turn to the God Self within. In turn, this amplifies the mass or race determination to demonstrate God, or love in action.

"Your freedom through higher, spiritual understanding is a constant beacon and reminder to others. This is an area where you really can throw your weight, since much help is needed. As to those sick souls who know better but attempt to become suppliers or sellers to others, there will be rapid karmic (cause and effect) payoff. They will be taught their lesson in short order so as to remove this blind spot and to get busy with their true Earth mission in this Mark Age period and program, which is the dawning of the Age of Aquarius. So be it."

AWARE YOUTH SEEK GOD

Beginning since about 1940 there have been incarnating upon the Earth highly spiritual souls who are infiltrating every culture, nation, race and religion to bring forth the higher Aquarian teachings and principles. To all in this category: if you each manifest your individual spiritual Self you can prevent crises in your own life, in your own family, in your own community, in your own country, thus bringing about harmony, understanding and peace on planet Earth. Are you demonstrating this in your personal life, school, family and community?

Unfortunately, some will not be able to adjust to the incoming fourth dimensional frequencies of our planet. By fighting against the spiritual Age of Aquarius they react in an emotional, imbalanced way negatively, with violence and separation from one another instead of unity and brotherhood under one God.

But meanwhile, thousands of young adults today are intuned with the present spiritual crisis facing mankind and the Earth planet in these Latter Days or the Mark Age period and program. They are offsetting the great negativity which many project out through drugs and disinterest in this dawning of the Age of Aquarius. Constructive activities by those who have eliminated the negative and are accentuating the positive include:

• The centers opened by young adults in many cities around the world to give legal aid and counsel to those in trouble due to drugs, sex, violent acts, and to function as go-betweens with established social-work programs.

• The students who, with cooperation from receptive court and city officials, have acted as advisors in city government and juries when youth–adult conflicts are being aired.

• The meditation groups being formed in homes, schools, colleges, churches to study healing, psychic development and other subjects of expanding awareness.

• The hundreds of bookstores and newsstands catering to spiritual, psychic, extraterrestrial and other occult matters about which youths are seeking knowledge.

• The tremendous upsurge of New Age music, writings, scientific projects and proper community-living experiments by young adults between ages eighteen and twenty-five.

SUPPORT THE YOUTH

On September 17, 1997, my Nada Self, in conclave with Sananda and others of the Hierarchal Board of our solar system, gave the following evaluation of the hierarchal program at this critical turning point. The spiritual awakening of today's youth–assisted through the mutual efforts of all I Am Nation citizens–remains a key factor in preparing planet Earth for the Aquarian Age.

"The score is barely over the fifty-percent equation for positive results. There is nothing to rejoice in this evaluation, because at-the slightest tilt and the slightest neglect, the most minor laziness can swing the pendulum into the negative column for the rest of this hierarchal program.

"The results of this evaluation have little to do with those who have dedicated themselves to the hierarchal evolutionary program which has been channeled through many and will continue to be channeled or realized from the highest I Am Self consciousness during these Latter-Day programs and the last battle in the horrendous

War of Armageddon. The swing vote for this has been the population of Earth incarnated physically of those twenty-one years old and younger. It is the consciousness and the soul determination of this generation that has cried out in despair and horror at the neglect of their parents and their grandparents. Many of them have seen the deterioration of siblings who are older than themselves due to neglect and nonparticipation by their parents and grandparents.

"The awakening of New Age consciousness or the hierarchal plan for evolutionary growth came in the sixties. That was the beginning of the Mark Age period and program. The opportunities given to those who participated in this higher possibility of life on the planet—to bring about *peace, love, cooperation and coordination*—gradually disintegrated into materialism and non-caring.

"We use the term *laziness* in the sense that those who started to see and to understand what was involved began to feel that somebody else, or that Spirit, would take care of all the problems they observed in other members of the human race everywhere on the planet and in the structures and power centers in all departments of life. They either joined those power centers or they let somebody else worry about or pursue the transmutations of those areas that desperately need change of consciousness and change of action, so that all can evolve *together*.

"This eventually became a popular notion amongst the so-called light workers or New Age advocates, that space brothers, masters, Spirit Itself would do the work and they, the disciples, the students of these subjects, would just be lifted along with the tide.

"The neglect of organized religions throughout the world, the neglect of the so-called enlightened to the needs for the planet to change, is the cause for the low level of energy coming from the planet, and does not provide a strong enough force field for those on the higher planes or even in the space program to descend.

"There is no ascension of consciousness, except in the very young, who have felt and are beginning to express that unless they do the *work*, unless they *unify*, unless they *express* these understandings and revelations, nothing will change—except catastrophe will force change.

"The key here, of course, is that no one does anything for us except ourselves. The awakening of such consciousness means work on oneself, not work on projects, objective impactions, and the criticism of what already is and has been the power structure of the planet for thousands of years.

"The only change that can take place is the change of each individual to bring himself or herself into alignment with the highest principles of the cosmos. For that is what the New Age represents.

"The Age of Aquarius represents the opportunity for humanity incarnated on the planet known as Earth, that it is to take at least two thousand years for Aquarian qualities to manifest fully for each and every individual, and each and every species, and the planet itself in order for all to be restored to healthy balance.

ASCENSION OF YOUTH
Key to our planetary future
"Reaching"
UNICEF photo by Antoine Desilets

"No one over the age of twenty-one at this particular time—and that's an approximation—can point the finger at any other one. For those who are in that youth bracket, just approaching adulthood, have no power, have no past history in this current incarnation which allows them to make those changes. It is always those who are of greater age than the arrival of maturity who have the energy, the power, the positions to bring about what is needed in every aspect of human life on planet Earth.

"Therefore, let it be understood that the focus for all those who wish to participate in the Second Coming program of individualized I Am Self externalization and the return, the redescent of the master teacher of this planet—who is known as Sananda (whose incarnations include: Jesus the Christ, Gautama Buddha, Moses)—will have to be centered around the support of those young individuals. Let it

159

be understood, of course, that everyone of that age is not of this consciousness. It is those with this consciousness of that age area who have made it possible to tip the scale a little beyond fifty-fifty.

"If they do not get the support from all of those above that approximate age bracket, they will not be able to accomplish what their souls and hearts and minds presently are telling them needs to be done.

"Programs which support and teach this, which encourage individualized efforts to become I Am citizens of the I Am Nation, which is to be established on Earth soon, are those programs which need and should receive the best efforts and energies that all on the planet are capable of giving.

"This will not be easy, for most have already ignored the hierarchal plan and program; therefore, it is not highly likely that suddenly they will see the wisdom of this evaluation. Most will not accept the source through which it has come, nor the need, nor the practicality of what is being presented here and evaluated at this juncture in the last battle of the War of Armageddon. But where there are *peace, love, cooperation and coordination,* an effort now can be strengthened and pursued.

"No one of Earth is going to be saved by anyone else: be it a master teacher, be it a manifestation of the light body of another individual, be it the visitors from other planets, be it the beloved Sananda/Jesus the Christ himself. Each one is responsible unto him/herself for his/her own evolvement. And through that, collectively—with *peace* in the heart, *love* as the purpose, *cooperation* demonstrated, and *coordination* mandatory—we will be able to bring about a new heaven on a new Earth. So be it in truth."

GLOSSARY

akashic record: soul history of an individual, a race, a heavenly body.

angel: a being of celestial realms.

Aquarian Age: period of approximately two thousand years following the Piscean Age. Cycle during which the solar system moves through the area of cosmic space known as Aquarius.

archangel: head of a ray of life in this solar system. First: Michael. Second: Jophiel. Third: Chamuel (replaced Lucifer). Fourth: Gabriel. Fifth: Raphael. Sixth: Zadkiel. Seventh: Uriel.

Armageddon: the Latter-Day, cleansing, harvest, Mark Age period immediately prior to the Second Coming of Sananda as Christ Jesus. The era wherein man must eliminate the negativity in himself and the world.

ascended master: one who has reached the Christ level and who has translated his or her physical body into the light body or etheric body.

astral: pertaining to realms or planes between physical and etheric. Lower astral realms approximate Earth plane level of consciousness; higher astral realms approach etheric or Christ realms.

astral body: one of the seven bodies of man pertaining to Earth plane life. Appearance is similar to physical body. Upon transition called death it becomes the operative body for the consciousness, in the astral realms.

Atlantis: civilization springing from Lemuria, dating from 206,000 to 10,000 years ago. Land area was from present eastern USA and the Caribbean to western Europe, but not all one land mass. Sinking of Atlantis was from 26,000 to 10,000 years ago; allegory of Noah and the Flood.

aura: the force field around a person or an object. Contains information graphically revealed in color to those able to see with spiritual vision.

chakra: a center of energy focus, generally located around one of the seven major endocrine glands, but which penetrates the other, more subtle, bodies.

channel: a person who is used to transmit communications, energies, thoughts, deeds by either Spirit or an agent of Spirit. Also called prophet, sensitive, recorder, medium, instrument.

chohans: directors of the Seven Rays of Life, under the archangels. First: El Morya. Second: Kut Humi. Third: Lanto. Fourth: Serapis Bey. Fifth:

Hilarion. Sixth: St. Germain. Seventh: Sananda with Nada. As channeled through Yolanda numerous times.

Christ: a title indicating achievement of the spiritual consciousness of a son of God. Also refers to the entire race of man as and when operating in that level of consciousness.

Christ, anti-: one who does not accept brotherhood and equality of all men as sons of God.

Christ awareness: awareness of the Christ level within one's self and of the potential to achieve such.

Christ consciousness: achievement of some degree of understanding and use of spiritual powers and talents.

Christ Self: the superconscious, I Am, higher Self, oversoul level of consciousness.

conscious mind: the mortal level of one's total consciousness; which is about one tenth of such total consciousness. Usually refers to the rational, thinking aspect in man.

consciousness, mass: collective consciousness of race of man on Earth, all planes or realms pertaining to Earth.

Creative Energy: a designation for God or Spirit or Creative Force.

death: transition from physical life or expression on Earth to another realm, such as physical incarnation on some other planet or expression on astral or etheric realms.

dematerialize: change of rate of frequency vibration so as to disappear from third dimensional range of Earth plane sensing.

devas: those intelligent entities of the etheric planes who control the patterns for manifested form in the etheric, Earth and astral planes, under the direction of the angelic kingdom.

devic: one of the kingdoms of God's creation of entities; see *devas.*

dimension: a plane or realm of manifestation. A range of frequency vibration expression, such as third dimensional physical on Earth.

Divine Mind: God or Spirit; in reality the only mind that exists, man having a consciousness within this one mind.

elementals: those intelligent entities supervising the elements which comprise manifested form in the Earth and astral planes, under the direction of the devas for those forms.

El Morya Khan: Chohan of First Ray. Prince of Neptune. El denotes Spirit and the Elder race. Morya is a code scrambling of Om Ray. Khan is a Sanskrit term meaning king. No Earth incarnation since Atlantis (despite claims by others), until as Mark Age or Charles Boyd Gentzel (1922–1981), a cofounder and director of Mark-Age.

elohim: one or more of the seven elohim in the Godhead, heading the Seven Rays of Life; creators of manifestation for Spirit.

emotional body: one of the seven bodies of man pertaining to Earth life. Does not in any way resemble the physical body, but has the connotation of a vehicle for expression.

ESP: elementary spiritual powers, the definition coined by Mark-Age in 1966 to supersede the limited and nonspiritual usual meaning as extrasensory perception.

etheric: the Christ realms. Interpenetrates the entire solar system, including the physical and astral realms.

etheric body: one of the seven bodies of man pertaining to Earth life. Known more commonly as the light body, the electric body, the resurrected body, the ascended body. Resembles the physical body, but not necessarily of the same appearance. This body can be used by the Christ Self for full expression of Christ talents and powers.

eye, third: the spiritual sight or vision. Spiritual focus of light in center of forehead.

fall of man: sons of God becoming entrapped in the third or physical dimension of Earth from 206,000,000 to 26,000,000 years ago.

Father-Mother God: indicates male-female or positive-negative principle and polarities of Spirit. Also, Father denotes action and ideation, while Mother symbolizes receptive principles.

Father-Mother-Son: the Holy Trinity wherein Father is originator of idea for manifestation, Mother (Holy Spirit or Holy Ghost) brings forth the idea into manifestation, Son is the manifestation. Son also denotes the Christ or the race of mankind, universally.

Federation of Planets: coordination and cooperation of man on all planets of this solar system, except as yet man of physical and astral realms of Earth.

forces, negative: individuals, groups or forces not spiritually enlightened or oriented, but who think and act in antispiritual manners.

fourth dimension: in spiritual sense, the next phase of Earthman's evolution into Christ awareness and use of ESP, elementary spiritual powers. In physical sense, the next higher frequency vibration range into which Earth is being transmuted.

free will: man's divine heritage to make his own decisions. Pertains fully only to the Christ Self; and only in part and for a limited, although often lengthy, period to the mortal self or consciousness during the soul evolvement.

frequency vibration: a range of energy expressing as matter. Present Earth understanding and measurement, as in cycles per second, not applicable.

Golden Age or Era: the coming New Age or Aquarian Age, taking effect with the return of Sananda around the end of the twentieth century. It will be the age of greatest spiritual enlightenment in Earth's history.

heaven: an attitude and atmosphere of man's expression, wherever he is. No such specific place, as believed by some religions; except to denote the etheric realms.

hell: an attitude and atmosphere of man's expression, wherever he is. No such specific place, as believed by some religions.

Hierarchal Board: the spiritual governing body of this solar system. Headquarters is on Saturn.

hierarchal plan and program: the 26,000-year program ending by the year 2000 A.D. wherein the Hierarchal Board has been lifting man of Earth into Christ awareness preparatory to the manifestation of spiritual government on Earth and the return of Earth to the Federation of Planets of this solar system.

Hierarchy, spiritual: the spiritual government of the solar system, from the Hierarchal Board down through the individual planetary departments.

Hilarion: Chohan of Fifth Ray. Last Earth incarnation was as Charles Fillmore (1854–1948), cofounder of Unity School of Christianity. Other Earth incarnations have been as Plato the philosopher and as Paul the Apostle for Christ Jesus of Nazareth.

I Am: the Christ or high Self of each person. Yahweh (Jehovah), in the Old Testament. Atman or Brahman.

I Am Nation: spiritual government of, for and by the I Am Selves of all people on Earth, to be inaugurated officially by Sananda upon his Second Coming. Neither a religion nor a political government, it is the congregation of all souls dedicated, above any other allegiance, to God and to expressing the I Am Self. Regardless of race, gender, age, nationality, religion or esoteric group affiliation, everyone is a potential I Am Nation citizen. On May 10, 1974, the Hierarchal Board commissioned Mark-Age to implant the prototype of the I Am Nation.

incarnation: one lifetime of a soul; not always referring to an experience on Earth only.

Jesus of Nazareth: last Earth incarnation of Sananda. Christ Jesus, rather than Jesus Christ; for Christ is not a name but is a level of spiritual attainment which all mankind will reach and which many already have attained.

John the Beloved: disciple of Christ Jesus; author of Gospel of John and of Revelation in the New Testament. An incarnation of Kut Humi, Chohan of Second Ray.

karma: that which befalls an individual because of prior thoughts and deeds, in this or former lifetimes. Can be good or bad, positive or negative.

karma, law of: otherwise known as law of cause and effect. What one sows, so shall he reap.

karmic debt: that which one owes payment for, due to action in this or prior lifetimes. Must be paid off at some time in a spiritually proper manner.

kingdoms: celestial, man, animal, vegetable, mineral, devic. Denotes a category of divine creation. Evolution is only within the same kingdom, never through the various kingdoms. Transmigration–incarnation of an entity in different kingdoms–is an invalid theory.

language, universal sign: transmission of messages, commands, energies or stories through higher plane control of body movements, especially arms and hands, of a channel.

Lemuria: civilization dating from 26,000,000 to 10,000 years ago. Land area was from western USA out into Pacific Ocean. Final destruction was 10,000–13,000 years ago; allegory of Noah and the Flood.

levitation: lifting one's body off the ground by spiritual or by higher plane equipment means.

light: spiritual illumination; spiritual; etheric. Also, God as Light.

light body: fourth dimensional body of man; his etheric or Christ body; one of the seven bodies relating to Earth living; the resurrected or ascended body through which the Christ powers and talents can be demonstrated.

light worker: a spiritual worker in the hierarchal plan and program.

Lord: God; laws of God; spiritual title for officeholder in Hierarchy; designation given to one who has mastered all laws of a specified realm.

Love God and Love One Another: the two laws which Christ Jesus gave unto man of Earth. The motto of the White Brotherhood, the light workers in this solar system.

Love In Action: the New Age teaching of action with high Self, action with love; the Mark-Age theme and motto.

Mark Age: designation of the Latter-Day period, when there are appearing signs of the times to demonstrate the ending of the old age. Also, designation for the Earth plane aspect of the hierarchal plan. Also, the spiritual name for El Morya in his incarnation on Earth as Charles Boyd Gentzel (1922–1981), cofounder of Mark-Age unit.

Mark-Age: with the hyphen, designates the unit cofounded in 1960 by incarnated Hierarchal Board members El Morya (Charles Boyd Gentzel) and Nada (Yolanda of the Sun, or Pauline Sharpe). One of many focal points on Earth for the Hierarchal Board. Coordination Unit #7 and initial focus for externalization of the Hierarchal Board on Earth in the Latter Days.

Mary the Mother: mother of Sananda when he last incarnated on Earth, as Jesus of Nazareth. Twin soul of Sananda. Her Earth incarnations include those as Zolanda, a high priestess in Atlantis; and as King Solomon, son of David, mentioned in the Old Testament.

master: one who has mastered something. An ascended master is one who has achieved Christhood and has translated or has raised his or her physical body to the fourth dimension.

master ship #10: mother-ship spacecraft of city size which is Sananda's headquarters for the Mark Age period and program. Has been in etheric orbit around Earth since about 1885. Will be seen by those on Earth when time approaches for Sananda's return to Earth as Christ Jesus of Nazareth and as Sananda, Prince of Earth.

materialization: coupled with dematerialization. Mat and demat are a transmutation or translation from one frequency vibration to another, from one plane or realm to another. Translation of chemical, electronic and auric fields of an individual or object.

meditation: spiritual contemplation to receive illumination, or to experience at-onement with Spirit or one's own Christ Self or another agent of Spirit, or to pray or to decree or to visualize desired results.

mental body: one of the seven bodies of man pertaining to Earth living. Does not look like a physical body.

metaphysics: spiritual meaning is the study of that which lies beyond the physical, of the basic spiritual laws of the universe, and the practical application thereof in daily life on Earth.

miracle: a spiritual manifestation, or a work. There are no so-called miracles possible, in the sense of circumventing a divine law.

mortal consciousness: the awareness of a soul during Earth incarnation, prior to Christ consciousness.

Nada: Co-Chohan, with Sananda, of Seventh Ray. Member of Karmic Board of Hierarchal Board. Present Earth incarnation is as Yolanda of the Sun, or Pauline Sharpe, primary channel and executive director of Mark-Age.

negative polarity: refers to the female principle in creation. The rest or passive nature, as complementing the positive or action polarity.

New Age: the incoming Golden Age or Aquarian Age. Actually began entry about 1960.

New JerUSAlem: the United States of America will become the spiritual pattern for implementing spiritual government on Earth in the coming Golden Age.

Om; or Aum: a designation for God. Means power.

one hundred and forty-four thousand: the elect, the demonstrators and the teachers of Christ powers during the Mark Age period and program. The number is literal, in that at least that number must so demonstrate to achieve the spiritual goal of lifting man into the fourth dimension, and symbolic, in that it does not preclude any number of additional ones from being included.

physical body: one of the seven bodies of man for living on Earth. Has been expressing in third dimension, but will be well into the fourth dimension by end of twentieth century. The vehicle for mortal expression of the soul on Earth. The physical on other planets of our solar system expresses as high as the eighth dimension.

plane: a realm, a dimension, a level of expression.

positive polarity: the male or action focus, as complementing the negative or female or passive polarity.

prince: a spiritual office and title, such as Sananda being Prince of Love and Peace as Chohan of Seventh Ray, and Prince of Earth as spiritual ruler of this planet.

prophet: in addition to usual meaning it is the term preferred by those of higher planes in referring to a communications channel.

psychic: refers to the powers of man focused through the solar plexus chakra or center. Not as high as the Christ powers.

realm: plane, dimension, a level of expression.

reincarnation: taking on another incarnation, on any plane or planet, during one's eternal life.

Sananda: Chohan of Seventh Ray. Prince or spiritual ruler of Earth. One of Council of Seven, highest ruling body of the solar system. Previous Earth incarnations: Christ Jesus of Nazareth, his last one; biblical Melchizedek, Moses and Elijah; Zarathustra; Gautama Buddha; Socrates, Greek philosopher; leader of Abels, in allegorical story of Cain and Abel; leader of Noahs, in allegorical story of Noah and the ark. Presently located in etheric realm, from whence he directs entire operation for upliftment of man and his own Second Coming; headquarters is master ship #10, in etheric orbit around Earth since about 1885.

Saturnian Council: Council of Seven, highest ruling body of the solar system. Headquarters is on planet Saturn.

Second Coming: refers to each coming into awareness of his or her own Christ Self, and the return of Sananda as Jesus of Nazareth to institute spiritual government on Earth by 2000 A.D.

Self, high: Christ Self, I Am presence, superconscious, oversoul, Atman,

Yahweh (Jehovah). The spiritual Self of each individual. Differentiated, in writing, from mortal self by use of capital *S* in Self.

self, mortal: the spiritually unawakened consciousness of Earthman.

sensitive: a channel, prophet, instrument, medium. One who is sensitive to or aware of spiritual realms and occupants therein.

Seven Rays of Life: the seven major groupings of aspects of God; the seven flames. First: will and power (blue). Second: intelligence and wisdom (yellow). Third: personal love and feeling (pink). Fourth: crystallization (colorless, crystal-clear). Fifth: unity, integration, healing, balance (green). Sixth: transmutation, cleansing, purification (violet). Seventh: divine love, peace, rest (gold and white). As channeled numerous times by Yolanda.

Son of God: with capital *S* for Son, denotes the Christ body of all mankind, collectively. With small *s* for son, denotes an individual. All men are sons of God and eventually will come into that awareness, heritage, power and co-creativity with God.

Son, only begotten: refers to the entire Christ body, which includes all of mankind, and not just a single individual.

soul: the accumulation of an individual's experiences in his or her eternal living. A covering or a coat of protection, over which the individual spirit can and does rely for its manifestations.

sphere: planet, realm, plane, dimension, level of expression.

Spirit: God, Creative Energy, Creative Force, Divine Mind, Father-Mother God, Original Source.

spirit: the spiritual consciousness or Self of man.

spiritual: term preferred over *religious* when referring to spiritual matters, as there are specific dogma and connotation attached to *religious.*

subconscious: one of the three phases of mind. Denotes the soul or record-keeper phase, which also performs the automatic and maintenance functions of the physical body. The relay phase between the superconscious and conscious aspects of one's total consciousness.

superconscious: the highest of the three aspects of individual consciousness, consisting also of conscious and subconscious aspects. The Christ, I Am, real, high Self. The real individual, which projects into embodiment via having created a physical body for such incarnation.

sword of truth: denotes the use of God's word and law to eliminate error, and to guide and to protect spiritual persons.

teleportation: spiritual power enabling one to move from one location to another via dematerialization and materialization, without physical means. A Christ power. Symbol for this in Atlantis was dodo bird.

tests, spiritual: tests of one's spiritual progress and lessons learned, given by Spirit, by one's own Christ Self or by other spiritual teachers. Not temptings, which never are given anyone by any of the above guides.

third dimension: the frequency vibrational level in which Earth and all on it have been expressing physically for eons. Being transmuted into the fourth dimension, which was begun gradually by the mid-twentieth century for completion in the twenty-first century, but well into the process by the end of the twentieth. Does not refer to the three dimensions of length, width and height, but to a range of vibration.

thought form: an actual form beyond the third dimension, created by man's thoughts. Has substance in another plane and can take on limited powers and activities, based on the power man has instilled in it through his thoughts and beliefs.

transition: term denoting death of an individual on one plane so as to begin a new life on another plane. Also, general meaning of making a change.

transmutation: spiritually, refers to purifying one's mortal consciousness and body so as to permit raising into fourth dimension, physically and as concerns Christ consciousness.

Trinity, Holy: Father-Mother-Son, Father-Holy Spirit-Son, Father-Holy Ghost-Son. The three aspects of God.

twenty-six-thousand-year cycle: the period of time, since the beginning of the fall of Atlantis, in which man of Earth has been given the last opportunity in this solar system for reevolution into the fourth dimension. Duration of a hierarchal plan and program to raise man from the third dimension into true status as sons of God. Cycle to end 2000 A.D.

veil, seventh: final veil separating man from knowing his divine heritage and powers.

vibrations: the frequency range in which something is expressing; not in terms of cycles per second, or any present Earth understanding and terminology. Also, the radiations emitted by an individual, able to be received consciously by one spiritually sensitive to such emanations.

world, end of: denotes ending of third dimensional expression for Earth and all on it, physically, and entry into a higher level of frequency vibration, the fourth dimension. The end of the materially-minded world of man so as to begin spiritual understanding and evolvement. Does not mean end of the Earth, but only entering a higher dimension.

Yolanda of the Sun: present Earth incarnation of Nada as Pauline Sharpe, executive director of Mark-Age. Was her name at height of her Atlantean development, when a high priestess of the Sun Temple, located near what is now Miami, Florida. Also known as Yolanda of the Temple of Love on the etheric realm of Venus.

MARK-AGE

Mastership Books

HOW TO DO ALL THINGS. Your use of divine power. Achieve union with your inner Self & master your life. Demonstrate your true heritage & powers as a child of God. By El Morya/Mark. **$8**

BIRTH OF THE LIGHT BODY. Master twelve spiritual qualities of your I Am Self, as symbolized by twelve apostles of Christ Jesus. Heal yourself. By Nada-Yolanda, with Robert H. Knapp, M.D. **$23**

EVOLUTION OF MAN. Origin, history, destiny of man. Major evolutionary cycles of Earthman in past 206 million years. Nature & powers of I Am consciousness. Channeled via Nada-Yolanda. **$15**

ANGELS & MAN. Seven archangels reveal nature & function of angels, unveiling cosmic relationship with & guardianship of man. Sequel to *Evolution of Man.* Channeled via Nada-Yolanda. **$15**

1000 KEYS TO THE TRUTH. Guidelines for Latter Days, Second Coming, mastership, karma, reincarnation, spiritual space program, healing, more. Based on channelings of Nada-Yolanda. **$7**

MAPP* TO AQUARIUS: *Mark Age Period & Program. Navigate the New Age with a tested road map for these Latter Days prior to Second Coming. Channeled via Nada-Yolanda. **$15**

VISITORS FROM OTHER PLANETS. Who they are & why they are here to assist our spiritual evolution into New Age. Federation of Planets. Mass landings. Channeled via Nada-Yolanda. **$15**

Mark-Age · P.O. Box 10 · Pioneer, TN 37847, USA